EMPIRES OF THE ANCIENT WORLD

Published in 1996 by
Marshall Cavendish Corporation
99 White Plains Road
Tarrytown, NY 10591-9001
U.S.A.

Editor: Henk Dijkstra
Executive Editor: Paulien Retèl
Revision Editor: Henk Singor
Art Director: Henk Oostenrijk, Studio 87, Utrecht, The Netherlands
Index Editors: Schuurmans & Jonkers, Leiden, The Netherlands
Preface: Susan Kennedy Zeller, Metropolitan Museum of Art Fellow, Department
of Africa, Oceania, and the Americas, New York

The History of the Ancient and Medieval World is a completely revised and updated edition of
The Adventure of Mankind.
©1996 HD Communication Consultants BV, Hilversum, The Netherlands
This edition ©1996 by Marshall Cavendish Corporation, Tarrytown, New York and
HD Communication Consultants BV, Hilversum, The Netherlands

Library of Congress Cataloging-in-Publication Data

History of the ancient and medieval world / edited by Henk Dijkstra.
p. cm.
Completely rev. and updated ed. of : The Adventure of mankind (second edition 1996).
Contents:—v.11. Empires of the Ancient World.
ISBN 0-7614-0362-0 (v.11).—ISBN 0-7614-0351-5 (lib.bdg.:set)
1. History, Ancient—Juvenile literature. 2. Middle Ages—History—Juvenile literature. I. Dijkstra, Henk. II. Title: Adventure of mankind
D117.H57 1996
930—dc20/95-35715

History of the
Ancient & Medieval World

Volume 11

Empires of the
Ancient World

Marshall Cavendish
New York Toronto Sydney

Empires of the Ancient World

Kublai Khan's Mongol Empire (British Museum, London)

CONTENTS

Preface

This volume covers the early history of such culturally diverse areas as Russia, China, India, Africa, and the Central and South Americas.

The Pre-Columbian cultures of present-day Mexico, Central America, and South America evolved in total isolation from any other influences, including European. There were numerous agriculturally based societies with complex systems of government, economics, religion, and art, among them the Olmec, 1500 BC to AD 300; the Maya, AD 300 to 900; the Teotihuacán, 300 BC to AD 700; the Aztec, AD 1200 to 1521; and the Inca, AD 1300 to 1532. These civilizations had similarities in their religions. Mesoamerica was also united through use of the same 260-day calendar. The Zapotec, Olmec, and Maya developed writing with the use of hieroglyphics. Technologically they were responsible for the building of some of the world's greatest architecture. The many temples of Teotihuacán, Tikal, Palenque, El Mirador, Copan, and several other centers such as Cuzco and Machu Picchu can still be seen. Sculptures, fine jewelry and pottery, and elaborate textiles attest to their excellence in the arts. Their very isolation contributed to their downfall as the Europeans in the fifteenth century brought with them deadly diseases, devastating the populations.

Wars, trade, and religion form three major influences in India, China, Japan, Russia, and Africa from AD 300 to 1600, as each area underwent several eras of small kingdoms, punctuated with periods of unification. India was the birth site of two great religions, Buddhism and Hinduism, which played a part in the warring politics of much of Asia and Japan. Other exports were more tangible in the form of goods traveled along the famous Spice and Silk trade routes. Allegiance to other religious philosophies, such as Confucianism, Muslim, Taoism, and Shintoism, contributed to political turmoil. Despite these wars, Asia had several periods, such as the Chinese Hsin dynasty, AD 8 to 105; the Tang dynasty, AD 618 to 907; and the Japanese Fujiwara period, AD 858 to 1160, where intense cultural growth was exemplified by the development of new governmental systems, poetry, literature, philosophy, and scientific inventions.

Russia was also subject to both internal and external wars and was not unified until Ivan III Vasilyevich threw off Mongol tribute around AD 1450. It was the Mongols, a raiding, nomadic, tribal group, who greatly influenced all these areas. Under such leadership as Chingiz (Genghis) Khan, AD 1167 to 1227, and Kublai Khan, AD 1259 to 1294, they swept into most of Asia and Russia, pillaging and destroying. The Mongols experienced one period, the Yuan dynasty, when they established a capital of Khan-balik and integrated the arts from diverse peoples. The Ottoman Empire was created much later than the Asian dynasties and its history is intertwined with that of Europe as the Muslim Empire maintained on and off relations in trade and in wars.

Africa also experienced political dynastic unrest as rich, culturally advanced kingdoms such as the Nubia, 1000 BC to AD 500; the Ghanan, AD 400 to 1240; and Songhai, AD 1400 to 1600, warred for power over profitable northern African gold, ivory, and slave trade routes. Other conflicts were caused by shifting immigrations of peoples such as the Bantu moving into East Africa and then South Africa, interacting with or displacing indigenous peoples.

Susan Kennedy Zeller, Metropolitan Museum of Art Fellow, Department of Africa, Oceania, and the Americas, New York

View of the ruins of Monte Albán, once an Olmec sanctuary until the Zapotecs took over the hill. Around 1300 they were expelled by the Mixtecs.

Pre-Columbian Cultures

Indian Civilizations in America

The great civilizations of the Americas prior to the arrival of Columbus in 1492—the Maya, the Aztec, the Inca, and several others—are all defined as pre-Columbian, divided chronologically into Preclassic, Classic, and Postclassic periods (from 1500 BC to AD 300, AD 300 to 900, and AD 900 to 1540, respectively).

Farthest north is the Mesoamerican area, today comprising Mexico and the Central American countries of Belize, Guatemala, Honduras, and El Salvador. The Intermediate area lies in the present-day Central American countries of Nicaragua, Costa Rica, and Panama and the South American countries of Columbia, Venezuela, and Ecuador. The

Central Andean area includes present-day Peru, northern Chili, and Bolivia. Despite the great distances between them, similarities in their art and religions indicate past contact.

Latin America

Spanish and Portuguese explorers followed Columbus at the beginning of the sixteenth century, when the Aztecs, the Maya, and Incas had reached their pinnacle. They had built cities larger than any the Spaniards had ever seen, with elaborate palaces, temples, ball courts, and magnificent sculptures.

Because the Spanish and Portuguese introduced the Latin-root languages that still pre-

dominate in these areas, Central and South America are called Latin America. Latin America, in turn, introduced the Europeans to items originally found only in the Americas, such as the hammock, llama wool, cigars, rubber, and food (chocolate, tomatoes, corn, potatoes).

Latin America is a region of extremes, from desert to jungle, from lowlands to some of the highest mountain ranges on earth. There are grasslands, tropical jungles, highlands, volcanoes, and deserts. It is generally assumed that the first inhabitants of Latin America were groups of hunters who entered the region from North America. They probably came originally from northeast Asia, over a land bridge that existed between Asia and North America in the last Ice Age. Signs of their settlements dating from about 17,000 BC have been found in Latin America.

People of the Preclassic era adapted well to the enormously varied regions where they lived. Those of the Classic developed great civilizations that both traded and warred extensively in the Postclassic years.

Pre-Columbian Characteristics

All pre-Columbian cultures were based on agriculture. Only the Incas had a beast of burden, the llama. The members of all other civilizations transported everything on their own backs. Most of these cultures were limited in tool technology, often despite great artistic, scientific, and architectural sophistication. Simple hoes were used by the Aztecs and the Maya for land elevation, swamp drainage, and irrigation. Inca terraces can still be seen on the mountains around the city of Cuzco, Peru.

The wheel was used to make miniature toys and models, but the pre-Columbian cultures did not use it for transportation or anything else. Their first buildings were probably of woven or bundled fiber or wood, then of adobe or stone, for which they rolled great stone blocks into place on wooden poles. Using only stone tools, they ground and cut the stones to fit together perfectly without cement. Ruins of Mesoamerican and Central Andean platform temples, pyramids, palaces, and tombs are still evident. Pyramids may have been occasionally used as tombs but, according to pictographs written on codices (codex meaning book or code) of deer parchment or bark cloth, they were built primarily for political and ceremonial purposes.

The pre-Columbians excelled in stone sculpture, mainly in Mesoamerica, and modeled clay figurines and pottery. They decorated utensils and sometimes buildings with incised carving, molded designs, and painted

In the area around Cuzco are a lot of mountainsides on which Aztec terracing is still visible. Using this system had the advantage that even the highest hilltops (as on the picture) were fit for agriculture.

Chimú vase portraying the maize-god. It was made in Chan Chan, a city that was founded between 800 and 1000 AD.

1448

Active volcano in Mexico

murals. While painting was common to all these peoples, the Maya, the Mixtec, and the Aztec developed pictographic writing.

Pre-Columbians worked gold, silver, and copper, including tumbaga, an alloy of copper and gold, probably as early as 1200 BC in the Central Andean area and, by about AD 800, in the Intermediate area and Mesoamerica. They alloyed bronze around AD 1200 and cast metal by the lost-wax method. They also soldered metal, embossed, gilded, engraved, and inlaid it.

As evidenced by samples preserved in Peru, pre-Columbians also wove textiles (primarily cotton or wool), and painted, stamped, and embroidered designs on the fabric. They used the wool of the llama, the alpaca, and the vicuna. Many of these textiles were considered by the pre-Columbians to be even more valuable than gold, with special ones used for ceremonial purposes.

Mesoamerican Cultures
The Olmec

The earliest of the pre-Columbian cultures was the Olmec, established on the coast of the Gulf of Mexico about 1500 BC. By 600 BC, they had developed a social and economic system that extended west and south to outlying settlements. Their major ceremo-

Olmec warrior

1449

nial centers were referred to as "the Heartland."

La Venta features a 100-foot- (30-meter-) high pyramid surrounded by platform temples and plazas in a parallel, symmetrical plan, laid out according to an astrologically determined axis. Teotihuacán established the first true cities as part of their elaborate civilization in the Valley of Mexico, with streets and areas of residential

Golden vase
from the Quimbayas
who lived in
Colombia

housing as well as temples and administrative buildings. The Olmec built the La Venta pyramids primarily from earth, but they also carved huge basalt heads 8 to 12 feet (2.4 to 3.1 meters) high that may be portraits of rulers. They set up several stone altars in each center. The Olmec also carved smaller, exquisite figures, masks, pendants, and containers from jade.

The Olmec set up other megaliths that depicted important events with picture writing. Their curvilinear art style is reproduced in cave paintings and in reliefs carved into the walls of caves. Here, as in much of Olmec art, jaguars with human features and humans with jaguar aspects are depicted. Tlapacoya also had a local industry, not related to Olmec style, of small clay figurines, some with exaggerated female anatomy and some dressed as male ballplayers.

The Olmec population, organized hierarchically, probably numbered some 35,000 at its peak. The common people, who worked for the leaders, were divided into two groups, farmers and craftsmen.

Colima, Jalisco, Guerrero, and Nayarit

Colima, Jalisco, Guerrero, and Nayarit are Preclassic and early Classic cultures of Mexico, named by archaeologists after the states where their sites have been found. They are notable for their clay work, effigy pots, and figurines, rather than any architecture. In Guerrero, Mezcala, small stone-carved replicas of temples and altars stand out.

Teotihuacán

The first city in the Western Hemisphere, Teotihuacán (Place of the Gods) lay roughly 25 miles (40 kilometers) northeast of today's Mexico City. The valley was first settled in 600 BC and became the sixth largest city in the world by AD 600. Most of its temples and some of the first apartment complexes were destroyed by fire about AD 750.

Teotihuacán was a state and city of exceptional importance for over 700 years. The city itself covered over 8 square miles (21 square kilometers). Apartments were built in one-story buildings constructed of local limestone and surrounded by high walls. Cooking was done inside on portable stoves set in the floors. Each area of Teotihuacán was divided into various sections of specialization, and hundreds of craft shops have been found in Teotihuacán's ruins.

The temples of Teotihuacán were an integral part of the city. They formed a giant cross in the center with major temples at the ends and several smaller temples placed along the so-called Street of the Dead. During recent excavations it was discovered that there is a major cave complex underneath the Temple of the Sun.

Murals cover hundreds of walls, including the one in the Tepantitla Palace compound depicting Tlalocan, the water goddess, with her hands outstretched and water flowing from her fingers. Plants and life grow from her head. All around her are symbols of fertility and abundance. The murals reveal little about who ruled Teotihuacán; perhaps the area was ruled by a body of the elite instead of monarchies. Nowhere are there paintings of any human sacrifices, wars, or battles.

Other arts created at Teotihuacán are the

famous stone masks, other jade and serpentine figures, and fine ceramic orangeware vessels.

Zapotec

The Oaxaca Valley people known as the Zapotec, originating about 1500 BC, built the great urban complex of Monte Albán. It flourished for a thousand years, from 500 BC to AD 500. It exhibits Olmec and Teotihuacán influence in its inscribed stelae, its platform temples, and the mural frescoes of its tombs. The ceremonial center consisted of a 1-square-mile (2.6-square-kilometer) enclosed acropolis, and several temples. The Zapotec practiced ancestor worship and utilized large burial urns.

Vera Cruz and Totonac

The Classic Vera Cruz culture developed on the coast of the Gulf of Mexico. One major site was Cerro de las Mesas. Its primary ceremonial center, El Tajín, included eleven courts for the ritually important ball game *tlachtli*. Reliefs depict the players in a series of panels culminating in rituals of human sacrifices.

Toltec

The militaristic Toltec lived in central and southern Mexico over the tenth and eleventh centuries. Their capital was Tula, some 40 miles (64 kilometers) north of today's

The temple of Quetzalcoatl in Teotihuacán, built by the Toltecs between 600 and 900 AD

Mexico City. Its architectural details reflected a social order enforced by intimidation. The pyramid at Tula is partially surrounded by a freestanding wall of stone serpents. Above it, the temple of Tlahuizcalpantecuhtli is surmounted by 15-foot- (4–meter-) high stone warriors that held up the temple roof. Nearby is the *tzompantli*, a display rack for the heads of sacrifice victims.

The Toltec either invaded the Yucatán Peninsula about AD 1000, taking over the Maya city of Chichén Itzá, or was an outpost of Chichén Itzá.

A vase from the late Chibeha culture, shaped as a man

1451

A chullpa (tomb) in Sillustani (Peru). This type of tomb was often built on the plateaus of Peru in the later centuries of the pre-Columbian era. Usually, several rich people were buried in one chullpa.

Portrait carved in a wall of the temple in Tihuanaco. This temple was built partly underground, and the walls are decorated with the portraits of people and gods. A couple of centuries after its construction, the temple was renovated. On this occasion, the broken or missing statuettes were replaced by new ones in the style of that period

Tarascan

The Tarascan prospered in much of western Mexico from at least 1000 BC to their demise at the hands of the Spaniards. Their capital was Tzintzuntzan, on Lake Pátzcuaro. They are noted for metalwork, textiles, feather work (the making of shields and headdresses from feathers), and their circular temples.

Mixtec

The Mixtec took over the Valley of Oaxaca in the tenth century, building Yagul, other new cities, and worship sites, notably Mitla. They are known especially for their mosaic work in masks and even walls. They were outstanding metalworkers, wood-carvers, and makers of the *teponaztli* (cylindrical slit-drums). Their pottery was found throughout Mexico by the fourteenth century.

The Central Andean Area
Chibcha

The Chibcha, an ancient people also called Muisca, probably inhabited the northern Andes long before the Incas they resembled. The Spanish conquered them on the Magdalena River, near modern Bogotá, Colombia. Although they built no cities, they formed an important society ranked from priest-leaders to common people, primarily farmers, craftsmen, traders, and warriors. They practiced irrigation, worked gold, and wove cotton cloth. Organized in tribes, they kept slaves, often sacrificed to the sun- or the moon-god. Since the chiefs wore golden clothing, the legend of El Dorado, or the Golden One, may have come from this region.

Tiwanaku

The Tiwanaku civilization arose around 300 BC in the *Altiplano*, the high mountain range of present-day Bolivia. It was an important power for several centuries but not much is known about the culture. A sunken temple and a number of buildings still exist near Lake Titicaca. The Tiwanaku created elaborate textiles and pottery beakers often shaped like animals.

Chimú

The Chimú kingdom flourished on the Peruvian coast over the ninth to fifteenth centuries. The ruins of its capital, Chan Chan, once surrounded by a wall 30 feet (9 meters) high, covers 6 square miles (15–square kilometers). Chimú farming required an extensive system of irrigation. The Spanish plundered Chan Chan between 1462 and 1470.

A reconstruction of an arch of Labna, a famous Mayan building

The Maya

Origin and Range

The history of the pre-Columbian people called the Maya spans three periods: the Preclassical, from 2000 BC to AD 300; the Classical, from AD 300 to 900; and the Postclassical, from AD 900 to 1530, when they first encountered the Spaniards.

There is archaeological evidence that the Maya opened their first ceremonial centers in Central America about 1500 BC. Mayan tribes developed in the Petén highlands of Guatemala, the center of their early culture, about 300 BC. Other tribes arose in El Salvador and Honduras. By AD 600 they were culturally dominant in those regions,

but left for unknown reasons at around AD 900. The tribe that gives the culture its name, the Maya, migrated to the Yucatán Peninsula of Mexico, the center of Maya culture, in the Postclassical period. Other Mayan tribes occupied the present-day Mexican states of Veracruz, Tabasco, and Chiapas.

Classic Maya civilization faltered during the late eighth and ninth centuries. The Postclassic Mayan, although never as powerful as during the Classic period, occupied major city centers such as Chichén Itzá. It, too, seemed to fragment by the fourteenth century, and an alliance of city-states, cen-

Early Maya inscriptions in stone, found in Tikai (Guatemala). Maya writing was not the most ancient in southern America, but it did lead to the development of the first mature system of writing.

tered on Mayapán, took over. The Spanish conquered remnants of highland and lowland Maya as well as the remaining centers when they swept into the area from Guatemala in the sixteenth century. Today, in all these regions, the Maya still constitute the majority of the population.

Agriculture

During most of the Preclassical period the nomadic Maya subsisted by hunting, fishing, and gathering. They eventually began living together in small villages and cultivating maize. They also started using slash-and-burn techniques to clear the jungle.

Left alone, jungle soil is fertile with lush green plant life, but when the Maya removed forest to make room for cultivated crops, they eliminated nutrients, then moved to another area and started over. This type of agricultural method determined the life of the early Maya to a great extent.

By the end of the Preclassical period those in wetlands were digging canals to drain marshes and building earth platforms in order to plant. Like other pre-Columbian cultures, the Maya of the Classical and Postclassical eras remained dependent on agriculture. They had no draft animals, although they raised dogs and turkeys, both probably for food. Work was done by hand

A chac mool (statue of a laying deity) with a sacrificial plate on his belly, made in Chichén Itzá. A typical feature of these statues is their posture of bent knees and a head turned aside.

1454

or with simple stone tools. Families worked land held in common by individual villages. Each local community had an administrator (or local chief) designated by the major hereditary chief of the tribe.

Maize was the main crop, but they also grew beans, squash, and cassava for food. Cassava, also called manioc, is a tropical plant that can grow 8 feet (2.4 meters) high. Its fat potatolike roots can grow to 3 feet (0.9 meter). They are the source of tapioca. Cassava sap can be used to make an alcoholic beverage.

The Maya cultivated cacao trees, using the valuable cacao beans for food and as a medium of exchange. They also used copper bells in lieu of cash. The trees grow to 20 feet (6 meters) in height and produce about 6,000 blossoms. Only about thirty of these form seed pods, which are almost a foot (0.3 meter) long. The beans inside are the size of almonds and are highly nutritious. The source of chocolate, they were introduced to Europe by the Spaniards in the sixteenth century.

The Maya grew cotton for textiles: spinning, weaving, and dyeing it. They made and painted superb pottery with elaborate depictions of activities of their elite rulers or of mythologies. Other pottery was incised delicately, and sacred cinnabar was rubbed into the designs. They worked gold, silver, and copper into jewelry and carved lapidary pendants, pins, and masks.

Urban Design

The lack of metal tools and beasts of burden makes Mayan architecture all the more remarkable. They had a standard design for their ceremonial centers, buildings con-

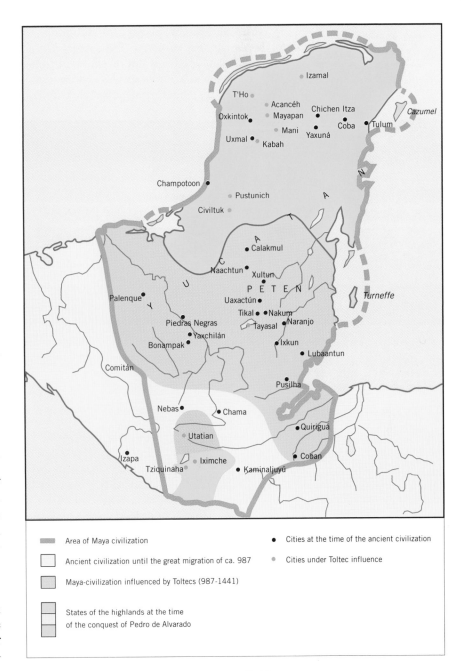

Map of the Maya Civilization

Pyramid of Tikal (Guatemala)

1455

structed around plazas for religious or administrative purposes. The centers had no streets and perhaps not even houses. No stone residential structures have been found, but there may have been perishable common

Jungle in
Central America

houses made of wood that have now disappeared.

The ruins of the ceremonial centers of Palenque in the Usamacinta River Basin; Tikal and Uaxactún in the Petén region; Uxmal, Mayapán, and Chichén Itzá in the Yucatán; and Copán, Honduras, follow similar site plans and have similar structures. Some of these are also considered cities. Each center has several mounds built around open plazas and topped with temples or palaces. Platform temples were built over cores of earth, rubble, or limestone, usually

bonded by cement, then faced with cut stone and plastered. The palace at Palenque, built in the Classical period in Chiapas, is typical. At 228 feet (69 meters) long, it stands on a pyramid of cut stone. These platform temples feature a mansard roof and a crestería, or roof comb, on top. Pictographs detailing the city's history are inscribed on some walls. On higher ground rise the trio: the Temples of the Cross, the Sun, and the Foliated Cross. In a tomb discovered in 1952, an enormous sarcophagus of carved stone contained the remains of Pacal, a king, buried in all his finery of gold and jade. The lid of the sarcophagus is inscribed with the image of the king at the moment of his death, falling rapturously into the underworld while the tree of life climbs through the center.

Stones, rolled into place on wooden poles, were so well cut and fitted that mortar was generally not necessary. The Maya constructed corbeled vaults, sometimes called false arches, by stepping layers of stone until they met over the interior. Walls were massive and generally windowless. Interiors were dark and very narrow. Possibly for this reason, the Maya painted them in vivid colors. They inlaid the outside walls with stone mosaic and painted them in horizontal patterns, alternating friezes (or strips) of decoration with plain stone. They carved decorations into the wooden door lintels and sculpted large wooden statues, painting them as well.

The Maya also built true cities with streets and residences, although none as large as their contemporary urban rival, Teotihuacán, in the Valley of Mexico. All cities had a central square, left open at the center. The buildings around it, temples and living quarters for priests, served a religious or administrative function. They typically included large palaces with many rooms and pillared galleries. The urban plan included ball courts, elevated causeways, and water reservoirs. Tikal had so many reservoirs for its population of seventy thousand that water was available even during prolonged drought.

Separate residential districts were built for rich and poor. Houses for the elite were built of stone, elaborately decorated and plastered. There is little sign of kitchens, leading to the supposition that cooking was done outside or in separate wooden (perishable) structures. The lowest-ranking commoners probably lived in wooden and thatch structures similar to those used by their descendants today.

The city square also functioned as a marketplace. The commercial routes of the Maya covered a vast territory. Tikal, for instance, had ties with Teotihuacán. Some villages,

Pyramid and columns near the Temple of the Warriors in Chichén Itzá

regions, or families specialized in the manufacture of a certain product, like pottery. The villages traded textiles, pottery, feathers, cocoa, honey, salt, rubber, wax, and artifacts. The highlands were famous for obsidian (volcanic glass), jade, cotton, gold, and copper.

El Mirador in Petén, discovered in 1930, was probably the largest city in the late Preclassic period. Its major temple, the Dante Pyramid, rises to 230 feet (70 meters). Another, El Tigre, is 180 feet (55 meters) high. The area consists of two groups of pyramids facing each other across a connecting causeway.

Chichén Itzá, on the northern Yucatán Peninsula, was the most important Postclassic Mayan city. *Chichén Itzá* translates as "Mouth of the Wells of Itzá," from its two natural wells and the name of the Itzá tribe of Mayans who inhabited it during the second phase. A major archaeological site today, the city was recurringly occupied and abandoned. It was originally built in the early sixth century AD, but was abandoned in 670, only to be reconstructed three hundred years later. The Toltecs seized it in 1200, making it their own capital and then abandoning it, in turn, at least a century before the Spanish conquest.

The city covers about a square mile (2.6 square kilometers). The main temple (to the god Quetzacóatl) is El Castillo, rising 100 feet (30 meters) from a pyramid mound that covers an acre (4,045 square meters). Unusual staircases rise on all four sides. There is a ball court for the Mayan ritual game of *Ulama* and a palace called *La Casa de las Monjas* (the Nunnery). Most notable is a stone observatory called the Caracol or Round Tower, with a rare circular snail-shaped staircase, built about AD 1050 by the Toltecs. They used a new technique of construction, setting square limestone plates over a rubble core.

The cities of the Maya were largely self-sufficient, frequently bellicose city-states by the Postclassical period. The Maya then fortified their ceremonial centers, erecting walls around them. Tulum, a walled Postclassic city on the northern tip of the Yucatán by the Caribbean coast, was the first Mesoamerican center described by the Spanish. It was built 1,000 years after the Maya civilization had peaked. After the collapse of Chichén Itzá, the Maya region formed a loose alliance with Mayapán as its capital. This was a poorly built center, derivative of Chichén Itzá. This too was mostly abandoned by the fifteenth century. When the Spaniards conquered this area they took over the remnants of a great civilization.

Social Structure
The investigations and excavations in El Mirador and other cities reveal that, by the end of the Preclassical period, Mayan society had evolved into a series of city-states that were controlled by a strong elite class. Its members demonstrated strength and gained territory by fighting wars. The conquered were then forced to work and to fight in the service of the elite. War improved access to valuable products from other regions. The Maya did not restrict themselves to the territory of other peoples. Those in the Yucatán warred among themselves, especially during the Postclassical period.

The more powerful a city, the more laborers it had at its disposal. By building enormous monuments an elite proved its power. Most stone buildings in a city were maintained regularly and were often completely renovated. The elite delegated both the building and maintenance activities to the lower social class of common people.

Mayan society was hierarchical. At the top, the priests, the military, and the political leaders retained power by making their offices hereditary. A hierarchy of profession was found among the common people, as well, with classification being determined by profession. Occupations enjoying more respect than others were placed higher in the social order. Archaeological finds of pottery, wall paintings, and statues reveal Mayan professions to include not only various crafts but music and writing.

Mayan statuette, made in the southeast of Mexico

Writing

No culture in Mesoamerica developed the art of writing to the level of the Maya. Like the ancient Egyptians, they developed a hieroglyphic script. This consisted of a complex combination of different signs and pictures, representing whole words, a syllable, or a concept. The script, not fully deciphered to date, was sophisticated enough to be used to describe details of astronomy, religious worship, and major events in history. It was particularly important in the recording of dynastic histories, or genealogies.

The Maya made codices, books of folded paper. Four of these, made of maguey plant fiber, have been recovered: the *Codex Dresdensis* (in Dresden, Germany), the *Perez Codex* (in Paris), and the *Codex Tro* and *Codex Cortesianus*, parts of the same document (in Madrid). These codices treat such relevant subjects as methods of farming and hunting, weather, astronomy, and illness.

The Maya used their characters for decorative effect, perhaps of ceremonial significance, painting them on their buildings. They also inscribed them on wooden door lintels and stairways and on commemorative rock monuments called *stele*. These slabs of stone generally were inscribed with the image of

Painted Mayan vase with a picture of fighting warriors, made in Mexico between 600 and 900.

Astronomic observation post in Chichén Itzá. The building is called "El Caracol" after the spiral-shaped staircase in the building.

The so-called "King of Kabah"

Jade bead
with a portrait of
the Sun god

the person they honored and a hieroglyphic inscription of his personal and family history, emphasizing his great accomplishments.

The Calendar

The Maya, although they did not invent their calendar, developed it into the most accurate system of chronology known prior to the European invention of the present-day Gregorian calendar. Most of the pre-Columbian cultures used a version of the Mayan calendar, two major calendars and a third one that overlapped these.

The first and oldest was a 260-day calendar, perhaps based on the human gestation peri-

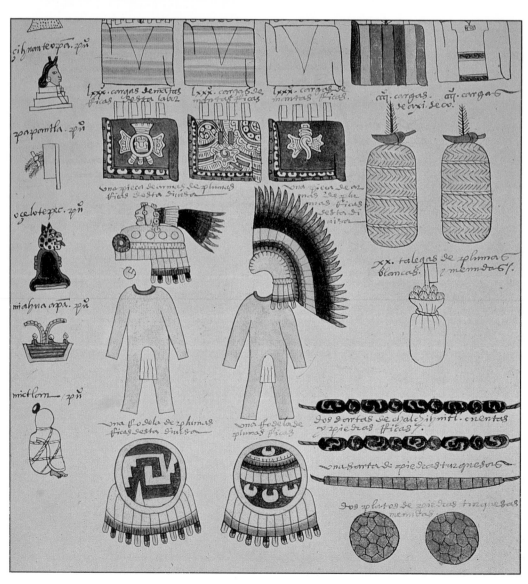

Page from the
so-called *Codex Mendoza*,
that was made in
Tenochtitlán between
1541 and 1542

od. It is divided into 13 cycles of 20 days each. Each of these days is given a number and a name, for example, one and monkey.

The second calendar was a true solar one that divided the year into 18 months of 20 days, with 5 nameless days at the end. These 5 days were considered dangerous. Since it made no correction for the extra quarter day, as present-day calendars do with an extra leap year day, this calendar always fluctuated. Both the 260-day and the 365-day calendars were set in motion together to mark time. It took 52 years for every combination of each name and number to be repeated. This was called a calendar round. The Maya had no special celebration at the end of the cycle, but other cultures, such as the Aztec, did. The Aztecs would break everything in

their households to start anew and sacrifice a human, whose heart was torn out and a fire built in his chest to signify the new beginning.

The third calendar was called the Long Count, used only by the Maya. Counting was figured from a mythological beginning of the world, a date which corresponds to 3114 BC.

The 260-day sequence had a religious function. With it the Maya marked rituals and their belief in the control of human action and time by the gods.

Religion

Mayan religion reflected the culture's dependence on agriculture and the forces of nature. The people worshiped deities manifesting those forces most vital to them. These

Sports field in Copán (Honduras). A ball was bounced against the sloping walls, and thrown through the stone rings on top of the walls.

included the god of the sky, Itzamna, and the god of rain, Chac.

Several other gods were also important: the Sun God, the Jaguar God, several so-called Old Gods, the Jester God, the Maize God, the Moon God, and the Death God. A major part of Maya religious practice had to

Statue in Copán, carved with hieroglyphs that describe historical events. To make a statue like this, a stone was set upright and fixed at the bottom and then it was worked downwards starting at the top.

do with the creation myth of *Popol Vuh*. It describes the origins of the Mayan world. Not written down until the sixteenth century, it was handed down orally for generations before that. The story portrays ancestors of the Mayan elite and their families as gods and demigods. The elite used *Popol Vuh* to convince the rest of the Maya of their divine right to rule.

The power of the Mayan religious leaders increased as the society developed. The priests acted as liaison between the common people and the gods. Because the Maya revered their leaders and often portrayed

them with godlike features, it is sometimes difficult to distinguish the image of a god from that of a person. To add to the confusion, the Maya attached great importance to genealogy and gave ancestor worship a prominent place in their religion.

The Ball Game

Ball courts have been found in a large number of Mayan cities. Some cities even had more than one; El Tajin, with eleven, had the most courts. The game the Maya played, *Ulama*, usually had religious significance. Images relating to the game have been found from every period; it was played in most areas of Central America.

Ulama was played on a stone floor flanked by two parallel sloping walls. The walls of the court at Chichén Itzá are typical, 274 feet (83.5 meters) long, 30 feet (12 meters) high, and 99 feet (30 meters) apart. A small stone ring, about 25 feet (7.6 meters) up, projected from each wall (something like basketball hoops). Two teams battled each other. The rules of the game apparently varied from location to location, though the main purpose was to get the ball, made of gum rubber, through the rings. Ricochets from the hip or shoulder off the walls were permitted. The ball had to be kept off the ground as long as possible, forcing the players to move about rapidly, often sliding on the ground to keep it in the air. They were equipped with hip, knee, and arm pads.

The game often portrayed an episode from the *Popol Vuh*, with the twin heroes battling the underworld. One of the characteristics by which the twins can be recognized in artistic representations are the ballplayer's shoulder and hip protection. The players also symbolized other important themes of Mayan religion, including death and rebirth or the cycles of the planets.

The game had winners and losers. The losers ran the risk of being sacrificed. To emulate the ball, the losers might be hurled from a staircase or decapitated.

A ruler might also use the game as a means of legitimizing his authority, playing it as the personification of a god or the

The "Templo de las inscripciones" in Palenque. This pyramid consists of eight plateaus with a temple on top. The building owes its name to the discovery of a stone inscribed with 620 hieroglyphs. Furthermore, the grave of a Mayan ruler was found here.

1463

descendant of one. He did not need to sacrifice himself in case he lost the game; he was allowed to pick a prisoner to die in his stead.

The ball courts were not designed for many spectators, hence it is assumed only the elite class watched the game. Since the matches had a religious function, in all likelihood the outcome was established before the match began.

Daily Life

The clan played a major role in Mayan societies. Each clan consisted of a group of inter-related families. Grandparents, parents, and children lived together, sometimes in large dwellings, but frequently in individual houses located in close proximity. The family was a self-sufficient unit. Most Maya were farmers who grew their own produce. There was strict separation between the work of men and women. Men were responsible for growing corn, beans, and cotton. Women were responsible for other vegetables and the turkey yard. They also wove and sewed cotton clothes, cooked the food, and cleaned the house. Large families were useful in working the land.

Before a marriage was permitted, the man had to pay a dowry to the woman's family. To afford this, the husband-to-be might first work for his in-laws. Once he had earned enough, the couple would move to his father's house to live.

Mayan dress was relatively simple. Women wore shifts, or loose-fitting dresses. Men wore loincloths. In addition, they would drape themselves in a type of blanket. The men wore their hair in decorative braids and painted or tattooed their bodies. Men and women also ground down their teeth, or inlaid them with gold and jade. In some parts of Central America, this custom is still practiced today.

Deceased Maya were frequently buried inside their own homes or in the immediate vicinity. Many such burial sites have been discovered in the ancient Maya cities. The dead were usually buried with some of their personal possessions. People of high station received more elaborate funerals than commoners, but all the Maya worshiped their ancestors. Dead ancestors were considered supernatural beings to be called upon in times of great need. The rich constructed large underground tombs where they depicted the life story of the deceased on stone. It is not certain if these were made to honor the dead after death or before. Some of them show evidence of human sacrifice.

Ruins of a temple in Tikal (Guatemala). Mayan temples always have a "crown" of stone and hieroglyphs.

Tikal, Guatemala. This city used to be an important center of trade that had contacts with the city of Teotihuacán in the Valley of Mexico. However, like so many other Mayan cities, Tikal, too, was left and eventually it was completely overgrown.

The Aztecs

Worshipers of the Sun

With breathtaking rapidity, the Spanish conquistadors destroyed the mighty Aztec kingdom. It took them only two years, from 1519 to 1521, using only a small number of men, to break the power of one of the world's great civilizations that had been two centuries in the making. Over the fourteenth to sixteenth centuries the Aztecs had built their empire in the central and southern regions of what is today Mexico.

The Rise of the Aztec Kingdom

The Aztec kingdom was born of an alliance among three city-states in the Valley of Mexico: Tenochtitlán, Texcoco, and Tlacopan. The Mexica who lived in Tenochtitlán were the most powerful of the three. According to legend, the Mexica came originally from Aztlán, in the north of Mexico. It is probable that the Mexica paid tribute to the Toltecs, who dominated the central plateau near Lake Texcoco in the tenth and eleventh centuries. When the kingdom of the Toltecs disintegrated and their capital, Tula, was abandoned, many tribes emigrated south to the plateau.

After the fall of Tula, the Mexica, too, moved southward in search of better living conditions. Their journey ended, after more than a century, at Lake Texcoco, an area that was then under the control of the Tepanecs. Latecomers, they were permitted to settle on a couple of small marshy islands in the lake, a location that other peoples had probably

Tlaloc, the rain-god

1465

Courtyard of the temple of Quetzalcoatl in Teotihuacán

rejected as a dwelling place. They piled up the mud of the lake bottom to make *chinampas* (artificial islands), which they planted. They built bridges to the mainland, canals to facilitate boat transportation, and aqueducts for freshwater.

For some time the Mexica had to pay tribute to the Tepanecs in exchange for the land, and to serve as soldiers in the army of their overlords. They gradually gained a reputation throughout the territory as good warriors and became a threat to the Tepanecs.

The Mexica lived primarily from agriculture, and their surroundings appeared to supply sufficient fish and game to feed the growing population. Around 1345, the Mexica founded their city of Tenochtitlán, on the site of present-day Mexico City. By marrying into the ruling tribe, their position in the state became stronger. They formed a league, uniting Tenochtitlán with the cities of Texcoco and Tlacopan. Together, they were strong enough to declare war on the Tepanecs and conquer the Tepanec cities.

Statue of Coatlicue,
the goddess of the earth,
discovered in Tenochtitlán.
The head is shaped by
two snake heads, the feet are
animal claws, and the
hands are snake heads, too.
As a decoration on her chest,
Coatlicue wears skulls
and human hands.
This goddess is the creatress
of everything, but she
also destroys all she has
created.

During a sacrifice to an Aztec god, the heart of a man is torn out. Drawing in the *Codex Matritense*, made by the monk Bernardino of Sahagun.

groups: the *pipiltin* (nobles) and the *macehualtin* (common people). Several subdivisions of ranks and classes determined where people lived and what clothing they wore. A person's status was fixed at birth and was the same as that of his or her ancestors.

The head of the Aztec state was the king, or *tlatoani*. The term means "he who has the word" in Nahuatl, the language of the Aztecs. In addition to a powerful king who handled the secular matters, there was an elected official called Cihuacoatli, or woman serpent. This male individual was normally dressed in female clothing during the ceremonies and held all the priestly power. It is thought that the king and the Cihuacoatli divided the power between them.

The king was assisted by the pipiltin. A new king was always elected by those from among the most talented members of the royal family. The members of the nobility were political advisers, administrators, and priests. They also constituted the military elite of the state.

The macehualtin, on the other hand, were farmers, craftspeople, and merchants. At the very bottom of the social structure were slaves, some captured in war or bought in slave markets. Others had turned themselves in to be enslaved in exchange for food and shelter. Any person who was unable to pay his debts, who had stolen, or who had committed a murder could be turned into a slave. As soon as the debt was paid, the slave became free once more. The children of

Aztec drum, made of carved wood

Around 1445, Tenochtitlán became an independent city. It grew to become the capital of an extensive kingdom, referred to as the Aztec Empire in the sixteenth century. Thereafter, the people called Aztec were very heterogeneous, consisting of nomadic groups of the powerful Mexica, Acolhua, and Tepanec, Toltec descendants, indigenous local peoples, and barbarian outsiders.

The City and the Society
The Aztecs were initially divided into two

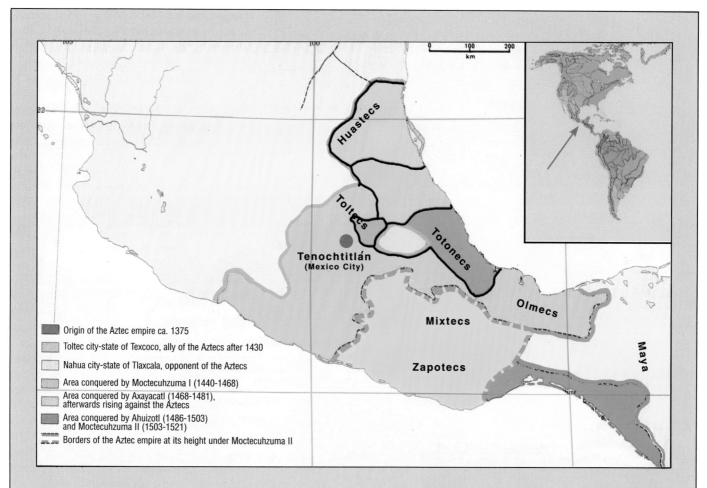

Origin of the Aztec empire ca. 1375

Toltec city-state of Texcoco, ally of the Aztecs after 1430

Nahua city-state of Tlaxcala, opponent of the Aztecs

Area conquered by Moctecuhzuma I (1440-1468)

Area conquered by Axayacatl (1468-1481), afterwards rising against the Aztecs

Area conquered by Ahuizotl (1486-1503) and Moctecuhzuma II (1503-1521)

Borders of the Aztec empire at its height under Moctecuhzuma II

The last days
of the Aztecs

After the Mexica overcame their rivals, the Tepanecs, they began to expand their empire. They made tribes that had once paid tribute to the Tepanecs subject to them. The Mexica oriented their new government entirely to warfare. They militarized the nobility and took firm hold on the country's administration.

The power of the nobles increased as the empire grew larger. Around 1458 the Aztecs embarked on a more extensive campaign of expansion under the leadership of Motecuhzuma I. His conquests were primarily in Mixtec cities and territories. He killed many of the Mixtec.

Economic motivation for Aztec conquests, always a factor, began to be replaced by reli-gious motivation. Since the Aztec gods required human sacrifice, the need for vic-tims grew. Captured enemies were brought to Tenochtitlán to be offered to the various gods. If the Aztec regime cannot be called an empire in the European or Asian sense, it is because it was based mainly on the desire to obtain captives for sacrifice.

Motecuhzuma I died in 1468. He was suc-ceeded by Axayacatl, who reigned from 1468 to 1481, and Tizoc, ruling from 1481 to 1486. The next king, Ahuitzotl, conquered large areas of the northern coast in 1487, tak-ing many prisoners for the gods.

A year after his coronation, he organized a religious offering to celebrate the enlarge-ment of the great temple of Huitzilopochtli. It is estimated that some 4,000 people were sacrificed.

Ahuitzotl's successor was Motecuhzuma II, the final Aztec king. It was he who lost the empire in 1521 to the Spanish conquista-dores under Hernán Cortés.

Map of the Aztec realm between the fourteenth and the sixteenth century

slaves were born free. As a result, slavery was not an important element in the Aztec economy.

Governmental Organization

In addition to this division into classes, the government was broken up into administra-tive units, the *calpullis*. A *calpulli* consisted of a group of interrelated families. Each calpulli was assigned a piece of land to be cultivated by all its members. They could also be responsible for a specialty skill such

The Aztec calendar stone
(*top*) and a replica in the original colors (*bottom*).
The sun is in the center — the
claws are the sun's hands
that break hearts. The smaller
circle contains the twenty
hieroglyphs of the calendar
days. Two huge snakes enclose
everything: the xiuhcoatl
of Huitzilopochtli.
Their tails are at the top, and
their heads at the bottom.
The faces of the gods
Xiuthecuhtli and Tonatiuh
protrude from their
beaks.

as salt making, mat weaving, pottery making, and brewing the sacred drink, *pulque*.
Each calpulli also had a temple and a school
of its own, where instruction was given in
religion and handicrafts. Young men were
trained as warriors. In time of war, the calpulli supplied troops. In peacetime, the
workmen of the calpulli had to serve the
public agencies in the city.

Expansion of the Empire
The Aztec Empire was divided into about
thirty-five provinces. When a tribe was vanquished by the Aztecs, the original leaders
were frequently allowed to retain their positions, as long as they served the interests of
the Aztecs. The leaders were even received

into the nobility. Their children were educated in Tenochtitlán, so that they could later
take over their father's position.

The provinces were obligated to pay tribute to the king. An official called the
calpixque was appointed for each province.
He was responsible for seeing that the tribute
due was actually paid. The method of paying
the tribute was based on the distance from
Tenochtitlán. Provinces that were close to
the capital, for example, were usually
required to pay in corn. Areas that were farther away had to pay their tribute in the form
of feathers, which were much lighter and
therefore easier to transport.

Economy and War
The merchants, or *pochtecas*, formed a separate class. More respected than the farmers
and craftspeople, they were equally obliged
to pay tribute to the tlatoani. Some merchants, unlike the other macehualtin, were
allowed to own land. Their sons were educated at the schools of the elite. All professions were dependent upon the importation
of materials from outside the city, but the
merchants had yet another important function: they were spies who traveled through
the entire Aztec territory and, on the pretext
of trading, frequently went beyond its borders. Since they could adapt themselves to
the ways of foreign peoples and speak foreign languages, they were able to do espi-
onage work in hostile countries. Later they
would report to Tenochtitlán what they had
found out.

The Aztec economy was based on agriculture and war. When the Aztecs made war, it
was frequently not to conquer additional territory, but to obtain tribute from the conquered people.

The Army
The Aztec state did not maintain a large
standing army. The common soldiers were
recruited from the calpullis. Military training
for young men began at the age of fifteen.
Until the young men had taken a captive,
they wore a tuft of hair on the back of their
heads. When they had taken a captive (possibly with the help of friends) the tuft could be
removed. After a youth had taken four captives, he was acknowledged as a full-fledged
warrior.

The Aztecs often fought at a distance,
using bows, slings, and blowpipes. It was
important to them to bring as many live captives as possible to Tenochtitlán. Aztec gods
were worshiped with human sacrifice, and
captives were used for that purpose.
Sometimes wars known as flower wars were

Aztecs who maim themselves to please a god. Illustration from the *Codex Magliabecchi.*

waged not to obtain tribute, but to capture as many people as possible.

The Gods

The religion of the Aztecs was extremely complex. There were a great many gods, all of whom could change in nature. This is called dualism. The Aztecs believed that four previous worlds and suns had been created and then destroyed. The sun of each world was at the same time its god. The fifth world was created in fire at the ruins of Teotihuacán. The central figure was the sun-god Tonatiuh. The fifth world, the Aztecs' current world, was predicted to be destroyed by earthquakes.

The famous "calendar stone" was found under the central square in Mexico City where the Temple Major had been. The stone is not really a calendar but a depiction of the Aztec cosmological beliefs. It combines a shape of the sun-god, Tonatiuh, with the depiction of the earth monster, Tlatecuhtli, with her clawed hands and knife tongue. Around this dual image are the symbols of the four previous worlds and their destructions. Thus the beginning of the worlds and their ends are depicted at the same time, repeating the cycle believed in by the Aztecs.

The great twin temple of Tenochtitlán was dedicated to two gods: the rain-god Tlaloc and the war-god Huitzilopochtli. Agriculture and war were of prime importance to Aztec society. The god Tezcatlipoca, called the Smoking Mirror, had a special function. He was associated with death, night, magic, justice, and battle, but he was simultaneously an aspect of other gods. The Aztecs believed that he perceived what was taking place in their hearts and that he knew all the secrets of the world.

It was also believed that the gods demanded worship with sacrifices, frequently human. The Aztecs regarded this as a duty.

Chalcedon knife, used at ritual human sacrifices to cut open the chest and take out the heart while it was still beating.

1471

Evil was averted by honoring the gods, since success in war and harvest alike depended on their moods. The manner in which the sacrificial victims were killed was determined by the purpose of the offering, the god for whom it was intended, and the time of year.

The Aztecs transported material on their backs, with a strap running over their foreheads. In the foreground we see two European knights in full armor.

The Aztecs made use of two calendars that had been in existence for centuries, both just as accurate as our present-day calendar. The first calendar divided the year into eighteen months of 20 days, plus 5 additional "dangerous" days, to make up the total of 365. The second, ritual, calendar included 260 days, divided into twenty periods of 13 days. It specified the days on which religious festivals and sacrifices were to take place.

Every twenty days a religious festival was held to celebrate the change of period. There were songs, dances, and processions. Human sacrifices were often required. The victims were usually captives from war or, occasionally, slaves. They were ritually washed, then beautifully dressed and painted in the style of the god before whom they were to die. Then the heart, still beating, was cut out of the body with a knife made of obsidian (volcanic glass). Women were frequently beheaded. Sometimes the victims were burned, shot with arrows, or hurled down from a great height. The skulls of the victims were added to the others on the rack that stood near the sacred precinct at the great temple.

The City

Tenochtitlán, which became the Mexico City of today, was the impressive center of the Aztec state. When the Spanish conquistadores came upon it for the first time, they did not know if they were seeing a dream or a reality. At that time Tenochtitlán was larger than any city in Europe, well equipped with roads and a network of canals, through which the inhabitants traveled in boats. There was a sewer system, aqueducts brought freshwater to the city, and enormous temples stood among the houses. Three dikes connected Tenochtitlán, which had been built in the lake, to the shore.

In the center of the city were the major temples, protected by a stone wall. The largest of them was dedicated to Huitzilopochtli, the war-god of the Aztecs, and to Tlaloc, the rain-god. Two great staircases led to the top and emerged on a platform. This was the shrine of the temple. On it was the stone on which the sacrificial victims were stretched before their hearts were cut out.

The houses of the nobility of Tenochtitlán stood just outside the stone wall. The nobles were the only people who were allowed to build a house with two stories. The rest of the city was divided into units containing either ten or one hundred houses.

Groups of citizens of the same profession or the same status lived in the same district. The professions were frequently related to the origin of their practitioners. Goldsmiths, for example, often came from the Mixtec tribe.

Daily Life

The vast majority of the Aztecs lived in simple houses, usually built of rectangular stones with a roof of branches. The houses often had no windows and the doors no locks. Less well-to-do citizens lived in oval huts made of stakes and roofed with reeds.

Inside, a round earthenware pot was used to store provisions. The beds were simple reed mats. Sometimes there were wooden chests for personal objects. A few luxurious houses had steam baths. The houses also contained equipment used for work and earthenware pots and pans for cooking. There was frequently a mortar for grinding corn. Torches were used for illumination.

Children and adolescents went to schools where they were taught good behavior and given instruction in combat, handicrafts, and religion. The Aztecs had extremely strict rules of conduct. Marriage was very important. Young people were taught how they were to interact with older ones, how they must walk through the streets, and what clothes they were allowed to wear. There were rules about the chores that a child might do at each specific age, even about how much food could be eaten. Outside school, boys were mainly brought up by

The Aztecs used toadstools that caused hallucinations.

their fathers and girls by their mothers. Girls were primarily concerned with household tasks and were subsequently married.

Clothing was designed to reflect the status of the wearer. Only members of the nobility were allowed to wear cotton clothes. Their clothes were often expensive and brightly colored. The ceremonial robes of the nobles were richly decorated.

Urn, portraying a god, who was worshiped by the Zapotecs

An urn, found at Monte Albán. The helmet on the head is shaped as a bird with a broad beak.

The clothes and ornaments of priests imitated those of the gods that they served. In their ears, lips, and noses they put pins and rings. They wore gold and silver jewelry, as well.

The macehualtin were simply dressed in clothes made of maquey fiber textiles. The men wore loincloths day and night. The women wore skirts that reached to the ankles and sometimes rectangular cloths that knotted at the right shoulder.

Meals, too, reflected the great distinction between the nobles and the common people. The Aztecs had no large domestic animals like cattle. The only animals that were regularly eaten were turkeys and dogs, found only on the tables of nobility. Exotic foods, like chocolate and fish imported from the coast, were also limited to the elite. The common people lived mainly on corn, beans, and peppers. The corn was usually consumed in the form of tortillas, much like those that are still eaten in Mexico and Central America today. Tortillas are thin pancakes made of corn flour and baked on top of heated clay ovens. The Aztecs also made an alcoholic beverage, *pulque*, from the agave plant. It was regarded as holy and drunk only by older people.

In addition to the food they grew themselves, the Aztecs in Tenochtitlán also harvested food from their immediate watery surroundings, including frogs, worms, and water bugs.

Agriculture
The principal crop of the Aztecs was corn; they also grew peppers, pumpkins, and beans. The techniques they used remained the same for centuries and were decidedly primitive. They had no draft animals and used a simple long-handled hoe.

As Tenochtitlán expanded, the Aztecs created new agricultural land from barren land by means of irrigation. In the marshy area around the city they also reclaimed fertile land by making raised island plots. They planted trees around the plots of land in order to prevent the earth from being washed away.

The so-called atlants > of Tula. Originally, these statues supported the stone top of the sacrificial table. Until it was destroyed by the Chichimecs, Tula was the capital of the Toltec realm.

Art and Technology

The artisans in Tenochtitlán were assigned to separate districts according to their crafts. Their services were of great importance in Aztec society. Headdresses and shields for warriors were made by feather makers from the feathers that were sent to the capital as tribute. Art was frequently employed in the service of religion. Sculptors produced the statues that were to be found everywhere in the city and in the temples. Other craftspeople included potters, tailors, and carpenters. Craftsmen made many objects from obsidian and greenstone. Masks and sculptures were made from wood, then covered in elaborate turquoise mosaics.

The most significant architectural structure was the pyramid, built of huge stones that were piled on one another in successive layers. The stones were rolled to the construction site on tree trunks. Without the wheel for transportation, a vast amount of manpower was required.

The End of the Empire

The first Spaniards the Aztecs met began their voyage from Cuba on February 10, 1519. Eleven ships with a total of 508 men on board sailed to the coast of Central America under the leadership of Hernán Cortés. The story goes that before these men set foot on his land, Motecuhzuma II had been troubled by omens of disaster. Comets were seen in the sky and a farmer saw what he thought were mountains moving through the sea, probably the ships of Cortés.

Cortés stayed on the coast for the first few months after his arrival. He and Motecuhzuma II sent messages and gifts back and forth. Motecuhzuma II's intelligence service gave him detailed information about the newcomers, with their beards and their horses, all completely strange to the inhabitants of the American continent.

Some of the Aztec tribes had not joined Motecuhzuma II in his great empire, creating significant division within it. That, coupled with a new epidemic of smallpox brought by the Europeans, which was deadly to the Aztecs, worked in Cortés's favor. He had conquered the empire by 1521.

The Spanish conquistadores demolished pyramids and built their own churches on the ruins. They destroyed books with the Aztec picture language and stole the golden jewelry, which was melted down for ingots that they shipped to Europe.

The Aztec ruins still stand, mute testimony to an extraordinary culture. Recent excavations have even revealed the main temple, Temple Major of Tenochtitlán, buried under the modern Mexico City. Nahuatl is still spoken. The legends of the Aztecs live on today.

An Aztec termazcal (steam bath) on a seventeenth century drawing

Pitcher, made by the Mixtecs. This people was very good at making ceramics and working gold.

1476

The remains of Machu Picchu, a good example of the Inca architectural style. The eastern part of this settlement was used for habitation; the ceremonial area was located in the west.

The World of the Incas

Lost Treasure of the Andes

The Spaniard Francisco Pizarro sailed with Vasco de Balboa on the expedition that led to his country's claim to the Pacific Ocean in 1513. He learned of the existence of the Inca Empire during later explorations in 1524 and 1526. A year later, Holy Roman Emperor Charles V gave him the authority to conquer Peru. Accompanied by 180 Spanish troops, he did just that in 1532, destroying the most advanced system of government in the hemisphere, pillaging the Inca Empire. At its peak it reached from the Andes 2,500 miles (4,022 kilometers) down the west coast of South America, and the people, familiar with

1477

Ruins of
Tampumachay.

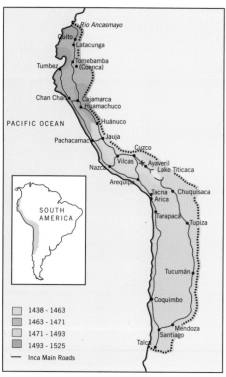

Map of the Inca realm
between the thirteenth and the
fifteenth centuries

advanced agricultural methods, astronomy, gold, silver, and bronze metallurgy, textiles, art, and architecture, had built great stone cities and stone roads and bridges.

The Rise of an Empire

Inca legends describe their origin through the story of four brothers and four sisters who left a cave and traveled to the Andes. Three of the brothers died en route. The fourth, Manco Capac, married his sister and settled in the region around Cuzco, which would become the capital city of the Inca Empire. This coincides with the anthropological version of the Incas. Members of the Quechua tribes, the first Incas, migrated to the Valley of Cuzco around AD 1100. Quechua was and is the language of the Incas. Recognized, like Spanish, as an official language of Peru in 1975, it is spoken today by millions of people in Ecuador, Peru, Bolivia, Chile, and Argentina, all regions that the Inca Empire controlled at its peak. Prior to the reign of their eighth king, the Incas apparently were not expansionist. That king, Viracocha, came to power around 1435 and conquered some 25 miles (40 kilometers) around Cuzco. His son, Pachacuti Inca Yupanqui, and grandson, Topa Inca Yupanqui, would greatly surpass that within thirty years. By the reign of his great-grandson, Huayna Capac, the empire reached 2,500 miles (4,022 kilometers) down South America and 500 miles (800 kilometers) inland.

War and Succession

Viracocha was an old man when his king-dom was invaded in 1438 by the Chancas. The Inca king had already chosen his successor, Inca Urqon, from among his sons, but Cusi Yupanqui, another of Viracocha's sons and Urqon's half-brother, had set his own eyes on the throne. Viracocha fled with his successor, leaving command of the army to Cusi Yupanqui, who would prove to be one of the greatest conquerors of all time. Cusi Yupanqui not only routed the invaders, he managed to take new territory while in pursuit of the Chancas. Cusi Yupanqui became king, assuming the name Pachacuti Inca Yupanqui.

When Capac Yupanqui made the fatal mistake of showing an interest in the throne, he was assassinated. Pachacuti Inca Yupanqui then appointed his own son, Topa Inca Yupanqui, as the new commander in chief.

The commander led his troops north and conquered the empire of the Chimú.

A desert people, they had managed to develop arable land using irrigation.

Fearful that the Incas would cut off their vital water supplies, they surrendered and joined the Inca Empire. Later, as king, Topa Yupanqui led his troops south to the tropical region at the foot of the Andes and to more conquests.

In 1493, Topa Yupanqui was succeeded by his son, Huayna Capac, who continued the conquest in the southern Andes, the equatorial Andes, and in what is now Ecuador.

The Inca kings had succeeded in vastly expanding the empire within a few decades. By this time the Spaniards had set foot on the continent. Their influence could be felt even before the Europeans knew the Incas existed. They had brought with them diseases that traveled faster than they did. When Francisco Pizarro first made contact with the Incas in 1532, they had already been weakened and decimated by the pox, a disease no longer lethal to Europeans.

In 1525, Huayna Capac succumbed, in all likelihood, to this disease. As was usual, the death of the king caused rivalry among his sons. Two of them, the half-brothers Huáscar and Atahuallpa, fought for power, dividing the empire into factions at a time when it needed all its power to survive. Pizarro and his 180 men had invaded the region from the north and begun their conquest.

In 1532, the brothers battled on Mount Chimborazo (Ecuador). Atahuallpa ultimately captured Huáscar. Later the same year, the vastly outnumbered Pizarro and his men captured Atahuallpa and made him a prisoner in his own house. The Incas had not opposed the Spaniards, apparently confusing them with legends of their Viracocha god who had promised to return from across the seas. Huáscar, though his brother's prisoner, was still alive; so was the royal rivalry. Afraid that Pizarro would depose him in favor of his brother, Atahuallpa had Huáscar drowned. He then offered the Spaniards a roomful of gold for his own ransom. (Another version of the story says the offer was one room of gold and two of silver.) In any case, Pizarro accepted the offer. Yet on August 29, 1533, while the Incas gathered the ransom, Pizarro had Atahuallpa strangled to death.

The Spanish conqueror then let Huáscar's

Part of the so-called Sungate in Tiahuanaco that was cut from one big trachite somewhere between 600 and 900. The head on top of the gate represents the god Viracocha.

brother, Manco Capac, take the useless throne. Manco subsequently revolted and was ousted. Driven off to the mountains, he was killed by other refugees. His youngest son, Tupac Amaru, claimed the throne, but the Spaniards beheaded him, ending the Inca dynasty.

Inca Society
Administration

The empire was called *Tahuantinsuyu*, or Empire of the Four Winds, and divided into four quarters: *Cuntisuyu, Chinchasuyu, Antisuyu,* and *Kollasuyu.* The capital of all four of these regions was Cuzco.

The quarters were subdivided into provinces and smaller administrative and economic areas. The smallest was the extended family landholding unit called the *ayllu.* The ayllu had both social and administrative aspects. Even though the land belonging to each ayllu was worked by its family members, its cultivation was supervised by the government. The government advised ayllus on crops, irrigation and drainage (including large-scale projects), fertilizing, and terracing.

Each Inca belonged to an ayllu. Each new king (the *Sapa Inca* or sole Inca) founded his own ayllu, which included his noblemen and a great number of common citizens obliged to work for them both. This royal ayllu was considered permanent. It continued to exist even after the king's death.

Mummy of a woman from Pracas, a peninsula in the middle of the Peruvian coast. This place was a *necropolis* (city of the dead) for eminent persons.

Painted earthen vase from Tiahuanaco (Bolivia)

1480

When the king died, his reign continued within his ayllu. All property and wealth remained the possession of the deceased king. A new leader, in order to be able to found his own ayllu, had to conquer new territory and acquire new wealth. Wealth was important to a king, desirable in and of itself, but also as a means of lavishing the socially requisite gifts on his noblemen. Wealth also provided his subjects the means to honor him in life and death. Kings acquired wealth through conquest and the taxes they levied.

Royalty

The Inca considered their kings not only powerful on earth, but able to retain that power after death. The royal family, which was named Inca, was regarded as semidivine. Inca society was tightly organized. The social hierarchy comprised the royal family, the aristocracy, government administrators, petty nobility, and commoners who were further ranked by occupation.

One of the recurring problems in Inca society was the battle that would ignite whenever there was a change of kings. The leadership of the royal Incas was hereditary. The leader, or *Capac*, would hand over power to a son of his own choosing. The problem was that Incas were allowed to have more than one wife.

The king's first wife usually was his full sister, or *coya*, reflecting the behavior of the founding ruler, Manco Capac, who also married his sister. In addition, he would have a number of second wives, usually selected from the elite of the lands he had conquered, and might have children with all these wives, with all his sons entitled to the throne. Thus, choosing a new leader was a difficult matter.

Ancestor Worship

One of the major phenomena of the Inca Empire was the worship of ancestors, to the extent that after death a person continued to affect the affairs of the living. Anyone of importance, especially royal dead were treated as if they were alive.

When a king died, his body was mummified, and he continued to live in his own house, surrounded by relatives. He lost none of his power and was deferred to as he had been when alive. His possessions were transferred to the *paqana*, a group made up of all his male descendants except his chosen successor. These descendants controlled his land and ensured that he lacked nothing.

The ayllu founded by the living king continued to work his land after his death. The king was regularly dressed in new clothes, received visitors, was offered food, and dis-

A ritual knife of the Chimús from northern Peru. It represents the god Naym Lap, and is made of gold set with turquoise.

Ceremonial
Inca plate

played on mats carried through the city on ceremonial days.

His advice was still sought, as well. Taking care of their dead king properly was the ayllu's way to ensure a prosperous future.

Taxation

The inhabitants of the Inca Empire worked for their own ayllus but were also required to provide labor to the state. Each healthy adult male head of household had to work a specified number of hours per year.

Some men cultivated the state's lands, others worked in the construction of public buildings, bridges, and roads, and others would serve in the army. While an Incan sub-

Remnants of a house in Machu Picchu. The Incas didn't use roofing tiles to cover their houses, but made mats of grass and branches.

ject was fulfilling his duty to the state, the government paid his board. The income from obligatory labor was used to defray the costs of the distribution of surplus food, a portion of each grain harvest from the allyus, in the provinces. No Inca starved.

The Incas had no system of writing, yet they kept accurate numerical records through the use of colored and knotted cords, called *quipus*. The imperial administration was kept by the *quipucamayoc* (people trained in the use of quipus).

Religion

Inca religion was a complicated affair. Its frequent and elaborate ceremonies were linked to matters of planting and harvest or medicine. Legends and music played a major role. In some rituals, live animals such as llamas and guinea pigs were sacrificed. While the Incas may have originally adopted much of their religion from the Tiwanaku culture,

they imposed their concepts on all people they conquered. Each provincial capital followed the example of Cuzco in erecting city altars. The existing altars and sacred places in use by other peoples were incorporated with those of the Incas and respected as long as the conquered people did not resist.

There were numerous gods whose characters and roles might change or intertwine. Together, the gods were seen as a spiritual force that ruled the corporeal world. *Viracocha* (the creator), *Inti* (the sun-god), and *Illapa* (the god of thunder and the weather) dominated a pantheon of deities linked to the forces of nature. These included the gods of the moon, the stars, the earth, and the sea. The Incas believed their kings to be descendants of Inti, the sun-god, who protected their empire.

The Incas venerated what were called *huacas*. Everything could be a huaca; it could be a sacred object, a sacred place, or a

1483

Inca vase,
shaped as a puma

An Inca quipu
made with colored cords,
which were knotted at
different lengths to indicate
a code

sacred person. The Inca world was full of them. When the Incas needed advice, they would consult the altars of the huacas. The Incas sacrificed children to the gods. Boys and girls specially selected from all over the empire, who were called *capacochas*, were brought to Cuzco at the age of ten. A special ceremony was held for them, after which the children were taken to the imperial altars and sacrificed. After their death, the capacochas were worshiped.

Assimilation Policy

The Incas conquered vast territories in rapid succession. Those who resisted were killed, but those who surrendered were largely left in peace. The Incas allowed the noblemen of a conquered region to remain in office. By changing as little as possible about the conquered people, they ensured limited resistance.

The nobles from the new territories were obliged to spend four months out of the year in the capital of Cuzco. The noblemen's children and some other relatives (usually brothers and cousins) were also summoned to Cuzco to become familiar with the language and customs of the Incas. Boys were sent to Cuzco when they were about fifteen years old and stayed there until their training was completed.

Status and Work

Status played a major role in Inca society. Everyone had a fixed place and function, tied to status. One of the most elite groups was the *yanacona*, men in the service of the king or noblemen, protected by the people for whom they worked. This released them from the obligations of common citizens. The Yanaconas were chosen from among the sons of the highest classes throughout the various provinces. They were trained as personal aides to the king, either living or dead. The office of the yanacona servants was hereditary, passed from father to son.

Another group of high social rank was the *camayo*, craftsmen, farmers, soldiers, or merchants who were employed full time in the king's service. They were exempt from taxes and were not subject to military service. Entire villages could be camayos, who were not obliged to reside at the court. Some continued to work in their native areas, which might be villages of weavers, potters, construction workers, or farmers. The king granted land to the camayos and provided their clothing.

Camayos assigned to specific work not done in their villages were required to move. Inca subjects who lived and worked in other than their native regions were sometimes

called *mitimas*. A mitima could also be a yanacona or a camayo.

Daughters of the elite were also eligible to be chosen for service, in this case to the king or the sun-god. The girls were selected from among the empire's most beautiful maidens when they reached the age of eight or nine, and were called *acllas*, or Chosen Women. Acllas were sometimes required to move out of the region where their parents lived. Parents were not told where the daughters ended up living.

The acllas lived in closed convents and were raised by older women who were themselves raised in the convent. A major convent was located in Cuzco, adjacent to the Temple of the Sun. Machu Picchu, never discovered by the Spaniards, is thought to be one of the oldest convents.

The girls learned how to weave special garments and to prepare special food and the sacred drink, *chicha*, for religious ceremonies. At the age of sixteen they were divided into various groups according to beauty. Some were probably sacrificed. Those chosen for sacrifice considered themselves fortunate as they were assured happiness in the other world. Others were chosen to live out their lives in the monastery in service to the gods. Still others were married to husbands chosen by the king, usually men he wanted to thank, or yanaconas.

Clothing

Inca men wore a breechclout and sleeveless tunic tied with a waistband under a cloak. The style of waist and headbands was prescribed by law and indicated a person's station in society. The common people wore clothes made from coarse wool and fibers while the nobles dressed in cotton and alpaca wool. The nobleman's tunic was woven with intricate figures around the neck placket. Most men carried a small decorated square bag to hold such possessions as cocoa leaves and small tools.

The fort of Sacsahuaman is about 399 yards (365meters) long and 59 feet (18 meters) high. It is built with heavy blocks of stone and no mortar.

Women wore long tunics made from squares of cloth wound around the body and fastened at the shoulder by a pin. They, too, wore sashes that indicated their station in life. Over the long tunic, women wore a wide mantle fastened with a large pin in the front, called a *tupu*. A noblewoman's jewelry would be of gold or silver while the peasant women used wood or copper. They also had a folded square of cloth on their heads tied with an heraldic band.

Cloth played a major role in Inca society. Pieces of cloth served variously as garments, shawls, bedding, and baby diapers. At times they used cloth as a medium of exchange, since it was easily carried and traded over long distances. Some communities paid their taxes in cloth. Soldiers and others who had fulfilled a community service were sometimes paid in cloth. Clothing not only indicated a person's status in society, it also played a key role in ceremonial life. For

Pottery with inscriptions and painted decoration from Paracas (Peru)

Fragment of a road, built by the Incas. The Inca realm had an extensive road system; by now, most of these roads have disappeared or become dilapidated, but here and there (as in the mountains between Machu Picchu and Cuzco) whole stretches are still to be found.

example, when a boy completed his puberty rites he was given a new set of clothes, and new clothes were fitted and given as wedding presents.

The Incas wove cloth from the wool of llamas and alpacas, animals abundant in the Andean highlands. They had domesticated the llama, which they used as a beast of burden, and hung bags on each side of the animal. The animals and their drivers often walked enormous distances on the stone roads, staircases, and bridges that connected the empire. The alpaca could not be tamed and had to be caught in order to be sheared. Alpaca wool, softer than llama, was in great demand, but harder to come by and more expensive. Cotton was grown in the capital areas and was also woven.

Remains from the temple that was devoted to the Sun. A golden statue of Inti and a silver statue of his wife were found there.

Stonework

The Incas built their houses, temples, bridges, and palaces from large, precisely ground blocks of stone, fitted so well that no mortar or cement was required to keep them in place. Testimony to the ingenuity of Inca builders are their many buildings still standing today. The carved stone blocks of some structures are ten feet (three meters) high and were moved by large crews of workers with pry bars over graduated earthen ramps.

Houses were grouped around a yard that generally had only one means of access. Doorways were tapered, wider at the bottom.

Windows were infrequently seen, but similarly designed. The Incas had few personal possessions, and their houses were sparsely furnished. A pile of rugs would serve as a chair, and the floor as a table.

Roads

A vast network of roads connected all parts of the empire. Used mostly by the army and members of the government elite, they also served as trading routes to the outlying provinces. Runners used them as efficient arteries for a system of communication that spanned the empire. The roads also facilitated religious ceremonies held throughout the empire. Where necessary, the Incas built bridges across rivers and ravines to provide access to remote areas. These included rope suspension bridges, one 328 feet (100 meters) long. They stationed guards at dangerous spots to protect travelers, repair the bridges, and prevent unauthorized movement of goods.

Machu Picchu

The real name of this Inca city is unknown. It was found in 1911 by the American explorer Hiram Bingham. He named it for the mountain that kept it so well hidden for so long: Machu Picchu.

Lying between two mountain peaks 1,950 feet (600 meters) above the Urubamba River, 50 miles (80 kilometers) northwest of Cuzco, the city was an engineering feat of some magnitude. It comprises steep terraces built around a plaza and connected by stairways. Most of its 200 stone structures have a single room, but some are larger. Just outside the walled area is a special stone altar called the *Intiwatana*. It may be a form of sacred huaca, perhaps a sun marker.

In all likelihood, Machu Picchu was a sanctuary. When and by whom the city was founded, nobody knows. It is located in an inhospitable region, during Inca times on the border of enemy territory. A network of neatly built stone roads leads to it, which was probably guarded by sentries.

The real role played by Machu Picchu is unknown, but many burial remains that date from the sixteenth century have been found in nearby caves. Since the majority of the burials are of women wearing fine garments and found with special pottery, Hiram Bingham speculated that it might have been a convent or retreat for the chosen women of the last king, Atahuallpa, who fled when the Spanish invaded. It also would have been extremely difficult for many people to have lived here year round, as arable land and water is scarce. Machu Picchu appears to have served a very special purpose.

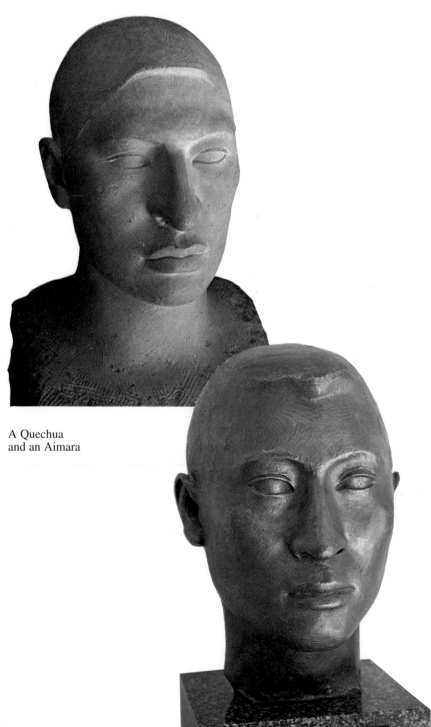

A Quechua
and an Aimara

'The bodhisattva with the blue lotus flower' in cave 1 at Ajanta; wall painting, seventh century AD.

India in the Middle Ages

A Seed of Civilization Flowers

The Indian subcontinent, the great landmass of South Asia, is home to one of the oldest and most important civilizations in the history of the world.

Archaeological signs indicate that since the early days of mankind the Indian subcontinent has welcomed human beings and aided their attempts at survival. To the north it is under the protection of the Himalayan mountain ranges, which also shield the landmass from the air currents and arctic winds of Central Asia. From the south this job is performed by the great swath of ocean, the same body of water that also seemed to separate it from the rest of the world.

India is roughly divided into two divisions, the north with the basins of the Indus and Ganges Rivers and the south with the

1489

A chaitya hall at Ellora; this hall is cut in the rocks and consists of an oblong room which is divided into a main nave and two side aisles by two rows of pillars; Gupta period.

Indian Peninsula; its borderlands are the Indo-Iranian on the west, the Indo-Burmese on the east, and the Himalayas to the north. Much of India's early contacts with the outside world took place through the northwest and northeast, where there is easier access by land.

A civilization is generally defined as a considerable number of literate people living in towns and cities, an idea that had come to maturation in Mesopotamia before the end of the fourth millennium. River basins, with their alluvial plains, are especially welcoming to life, and it was in India's river basins that two major phases of urban life arose: the civilization of the Indus Valley at the end of the third millennium BC and that of the Ganges during the first millennium BC.

During the third century AD, Indian culture reached its so-called Classical period. Despite all the invasions, all the wars, despite the chaos of the time, the arts and sciences in India attained heretofore unknown heights. This was made possible by the foreign invaders, such as the Kushans, who conquered large portions of the Indian subcontinent, and by the fact that those who founded their own Indian empires were receptive and not hostile to the rich culture they conquered.

The North

Throughout the third century AD, India had limited political stability. The situation changed in the fourth century AD when the Gupta dynasty came to power. The Guptas came to power as the Kushans, a foreign dynasty of Central Asian origin, were losing power in the north and northwest of India. Although their origins are unclear, the Guptas, like the Mauryas (a dynasty ruling the north of India from about 321 to 185 BC) were native to India. In AD 320 the patriarch of the family, Chandra Gupta I, ascended the throne. His son Samudra Gupta was a great conqueror who, from about AD 335 to 375, was able to build on his father's solid foundation. Within a relatively short time the Guptas controlled the major portion of northern India, while Assam, Nepal, the Punjab, and an enormous part of the south paid tribute. The Gupta Empire reached its zenith under Samudra Gupta's son Chandra Gupta II (AD 375–414). Literature, written in Sanskrit, flowered with the works of poets such as Kalidasa. Artisans painted splendid murals and carved great sculptures, architects built temples, mathematicians introduced the metric system and the essential concept of "zero."

Shortly after AD 470 a horde of horsemen invaded India from the north as the Indo-Aryans had done long before them. These were the feared White Huns. The Guptas repelled them only with great difficulty. King Skanda Gupta managed to save his empire by a hair, but not his dynasty. The family lost its power. The empire fragmented into many small states. The White Huns made use of this chaos by carrying out new forays into northern India. At around 510 their leader, Toramana, penetrated even further south. Yet the rule of the White Huns did not last long. Fifteen years after their major victory a group of northern princes drove them out of India.

Northern India was unable to achieve unity. Following the invasions by the White Huns, an era began in the fifth century that one could compare to the Middle Ages in Europe. Only at the beginning of the seventh century, from 606 to 647, was the remarkable Buddhist king Harsha able to reconnect parts of the Gupta Empire. This new empire did not long survive its founder. It would take another century for the political situation to stabilize.

In the meantime, two major powers came into being. In the region of Bengal, in the east, the Pala dynasty rose to power. These were Buddhists who would control the area well into the twelfth century. In the north-

west, the Rajputs, interrelated clans of fearsome warriors ruled by a military aristocracy, were making themselves heard. No one knows where they came from, but legend has it that four families were born of a sacrificial fire on the sacred mountain of Abu. More likely, they descended from either the Huns

who settled in northern and western India or from various other peoples who came in with the Huns.

The Muslims reached India, and after the death of Prophet Muhammad in 632, millions were converted to the new religion. The Prophet's followers represented an awesome political force. The conquest of Sind in 712 by Arabs had made this clear to everyone. At first the Muslim sphere of influence was limited to the Indus plain. The Muslims encoun-

A Buddha from the Gupta period; the right hand (cut off) makes the sign of fearlessness

tered great resistance from the Hindu princes in the north, particularly the Rajputs.

Toward the end of the tenth century, the power of the Rajputs waned. As before, the country was divided into factions warring against each other. Mahmud of Ghazni, a Turkish nobleman ruling from Afghanistan, used this to his advantage by occupying the Punjab and making yearly raids into India from about 1004 until his death in 1030.

The South

The southern part of the subcontinent had been united in the third century BC under the Maurya. The regions of the Deccan plateau and the rest of the south went their separate ways after the death of Emperor Asóka in 232 BC. Up to that time, the history of those areas of India is characterized by a succession of tiny principalities.

Later, two major empires arose in the south: one on the Deccan plain, the other in the land of the Tamil.

During the sixth century, the Chalukya dynasty had become firmly settled in Deccan. The dynasty's foremost ruler was Pulakeshin II (reigning from 608 to 642) who expanded the borders in all directions. In the north, he ran into King Harsha, who successfully defended his empire. Pulakeshin encountered far weaker enemies to the south and east, but he was defeated and killed. His victors were unable to fully destroy his empire, and his descendants remained in power for another century.

In 757 the Rasthrakuta dynasty came to power in Deccan. They were excellent soldiers, unrelenting in their violent attacks on their neighbors to the north and south. The Muslims were to profit most from the chaos

A gilded
bronze statue from
the Pala period

A cave temple
at Ellora, cut about the
eighth century

1492

they caused. The Deccan Hindu kings continued to rule until 1190, when the empire was fragmented by the onslaught of Muslim aggression.

In the extreme south, the Tamil preserved their independence as well as their Dravida culture. Ultimately, they were forced to become subject to the Hindu Pallava dynasty from the north.

The Pallavas continued to rule until the end of the ninth century, when their former vassals, the Chola, destroyed their power base. The Chola, in turn, founded an empire that comprised all of southern India and Sri Lanka. At times their armies advanced as far north as the Ganges River. In the early eleventh century the Chola navy under King Rajendra I was the largest ever to sail the Indian Ocean. He even outfitted an expedition to the Indonesian archipelago and Malaysia.

In 1216 the Pandya dynasty toppled the

One of the five seventh-century temples in Mamallapuram (near Madras). These five temples are built in the shape of a wagon (ratha) and hewn from granite.

Temple dedicated to Mukteshvara at Bhubaneshwar, built around the end of the tenth and the beginning of the eleventh century.

weakened regime of the Chola, but its reign was relatively short-lived compared to those of its predecessors. It was unable to withstand the invasions of the south by the troops of the Afghan Khalji Sultan of Delhi in 1310. Pandya rule was over. Most of India was now in the hands of the Muslims.

The Muslims in India

The conquest of India by various Muslim rulers took centuries. The immense size of the subcontinent had much to do with it. The Islamic troops had to battle powerful kingdoms that together exceeded the size of Europe. Initially the Muslims took hold only in the northwest, in the Indus delta.

The first contact with Islam came in the seventh century through Arab traders whose ships landed on the west coast of India. These early contacts were peaceful, with some Arabs intermarrying into local Rajput families. In 711, however, the plundering of Arab ships by Indian pirates caused the Ummayad governor of Iraq to launch an attack against the maharajas of Sind in modern Pakistan.

After the conquest of Sind in 712, it would not be until the tenth century that Islam would spread to other areas of the Indian subcontinent with various Turk or Afghan groups traveling across the Khyber Pass in the subsequent centuries.

One of the earliest of these incursions into India was by Mahmud of Ghazni (reigned

The Kuth minaret is part of the mosque, construction of which was started under Kuth ad-Bin and completed under his successors. The minaret is decorated with Hindu motives.

Relief of the Rajarani temple at Bhubaneswar, built at the end of the tenth century

Hindu stele
from the twelfth century
representing the god
Vishnu

998–1030). Descended from Turkish and Central Asian nomads driven into Persia and Afghanistan by the western expansion of China, Mahmud made at least seventeen annual expeditions into India from his capital in Ghazni, in Afghanistan. His nominal territory extended from Persia (Iran) to the Ganges River. Nevertheless, his actual control in India was not notable. He only controlled the northern frontier regions through his annual expeditions there.

Somnath

One of Mahmud's expeditions deserves special mention. He dispatched his troops to the great Hindu temple of Somnath. A large iron lingam was kept there (a sculpted symbol of the Hindu god Shiva). According to a thirteenth-century Arab source, the lingam was washed daily with water from the sacred Ganges. More than 1,000 carriers brought the water every day. The statue was worshiped by 1,000 Brahmans and 600 musicians, dancers, and servants. The temple had 10,000 settlements that gave their income to the deity, in addition to the offerings made by countless pilgrims. As an orthodox Muslim, Mahmud considered the Hindu temple as a place dedicated to idol worship, so he had the temple razed. He looted the temple's great wealth and had it taken to his treasury in Ghazni. His soldiers massacred the 50,000 Hindus who attempted to defend their sanctuary.

Muhammad of Ghur

Great dissension among the Turk and Afghan rulers and nobles of northern India frequently led to battle. In the twelfth century, Muhammad of Ghur decided to conquer the region to end internal feuds and establish a true Islamic empire. He did so. By 1192 he had also conquered the Hindu empire of Delhi.

The Slave Sultans of Delhi

Muhammad of Ghur was assassinated in 1206. The empire he had established around Delhi would continue to exist until 1526, with successive Turko-Afghan dynasties, the Khaljis, Tughluqs, Sayyids, and Losis. After Muhammad's death, his general, Qutb al-Din Aybak, took over, declaring himself sultan of Delhi and founding the dynasty of the "Slave" sultans. The "Slave" sultanate, which lasted until 1290, derived its name from the fact that many of the rulers were slaves or children of slaves who converted to Islam, entered military service, and later rose to prominence.

Most subjects of the Delhi sultans, however, were Hindus who were unwilling to accept Muslim hegemony. Time and again

Siva and his wife Parvati, made between the twelfth and thirteenth century

the Islamic rulers crushed uprisings. Only in regions where they had garrisons and fortifications did any measure of stability exist. The Delhi sultans could never afford to alienate any secondary Hindu leaders.

At about 1330 the Delhi sultanate reached its greatest extension under the Tughluqs. From 1327 to 1330 Sultan Muhammad Ibn Tughluq (reigned 1325–51) moved the capital from Delhi to the city of Daulatabad on the Deccan plateau. Since it was more centrally located, Muhammad thought he would be able to control the southern provinces. Yet he was unsuccessful in forging the empire into a single unit and slowly many provincial governors and nobles rebelled, setting up their own independent sultanates, such as the Shahi dynasty in Bengal, which declared independence from Delhi in 1338, and the Bahmani dynasty of the Deccan plateau, founded in 1347.

The Tughluq dynasty came to a close in 1398, with the devastating sack of Delhi by the Mongol ruler of Samarkand, Timur, known in the west as Tamerlane. This left the Delhi sultans in control of little more than the city of Delhi and its immediate vicinity. Although the sultanate later reconquered some of its former territories, the rulers resigned themselves to the purely nominal acknowledgment of their supremacy in India.

In April 1526, the last Delhi sultan, Ibrahim Lodi, was defeated near Panipat, north of Delhi, by Babur, founder of the Mughal dynasty in India. With minor interruptions, the Mughals would rule much of India until the middle of the eighteenth century.

In the Deccan, about 1400, the Bahmani sultanate had split into five states in the south, Bijapur, Golconda, Ahmednagar, Bidar, and Berar. The newly formed Islamic kingdoms of the northern Deccan were often at war with their neighbor to the south, the Hindu kingdom of Vijayanagar (founded in 1336). To resist the tremendous force of attacks from Vijayanagar, four of the Deccan kingdoms reunited in 1564 and destroyed the southern power. Although successful in the war against Vijayanagar, the Deccan sultans were exhausted and depleted of resources, which led the way for their later defeat and absorption into the Mughal Empire in 1687.

The age of the sultans had great influence on Indian society. Muslims and Hindus asso-

ciated with each other to some extent, and some of the sultanate rulers even exercised a more tolerant attitude toward other beliefs. Sanskrit lost its position as the official language, enabling a number of the regional Indian languages to evolve.

India and the World Beyond

India was in contact with the outside world, even in ancient times. Its influence was enormous. At least two world religions (Hinduism and Buddhism) were born on Indian soil. The subcontinent enjoyed renown as a land of wonders, exotic trade products, and immeasurable riches. Its land trading routes (the Spice Route and the Silk Road) were possibly the world's oldest.

There were also the sea routes. Off the Coromandel coast along India's southeastern shore, Roman, Persian, and Arabian ships anchored. They loaded products from China (silk and precious furs) and unloaded the products of Greece, Rome, Persia, and Egypt. This trade made the cities on the Indi-

A bodhisattva decorated with diadem and jewelery

Temple dedicated to Siva in Halebid from the Hoysala period (twelfth – fourteenth centuries). As the Muslims were on their campaign of conquest, the towers have never been completed.

an Ocean the crossroads of greatly diverse cultures and the marketplace for the world.

Regular traffic requires peaceful times, and both land and sea trade routes were affected by external factors. If a land traversed by the Silk Road suffered political instability, communications were severed that often took years to restore. The sea route was politically safer, but subject to violent storms and piracy.

Rome, a Major Trading Partner

At the beginning of the first millennium, circumstances were quite favorable for international merchants. Roughly speaking, only four empires lay between Gibraltar and Canton: Rome, Parthia, the Kushan state of northern India, and China.

With its penchant for luxury goods, Rome constituted an excellent trading partner for India. The Romans established a number of trade centers on the subcontinent, reaching as far as remote Pondicherry on the southeastern coast. (This explains the discovery of

a fair number of Roman coins both in north and south India and on Sri Lanka.)

The Articles of Trade

Rome bought a great many articles from India: Chinese silk, muslin (much in demand and of so fine a quality that it was called "mist"), gems (sapphires, rubies, emeralds, and diamonds), pearls, whole cargoes of animals (tigers, lions, the now extinct Indian bears, panthers, elephants, buffalo, peacocks, gold-colored parrots, and pheasant).

Indian spices and medicine included: pepper, palm oil, and cinnamon (often used in the manufacture of perfume and other cosmetics, in which the Indians had developed great expertise). Indian cooks were held in such high esteem that the emperor of Byzantium employed them in his kitchens.

The Cost of Trade

The Indians required the Romans to pay in gold ingots, a fact that contributed greatly to the impoverishment of the west. Even with

Gopuram or gate of
the Varadaraja Swami temple
in Kanchipuram,
the construction of which
was started in
the fourteenth century.

the exports of tin, ceramics, coral, and female slaves combined, Roman exports were minor compared to their imports from India.

The works of the Roman author Pliny (AD 61–114) deal with the amount of money exchanged in the trade between Rome and India. No less than 50 million *sestertii* (a unit of value in ancient Rome) disappeared into the pockets of Indian merchants yearly. In an apparent attempt to safeguard this trade with India, Emperor Nero, who reigned from AD

The Great Gate (Mongolian) in Delhi. When the Mongol period started in 1526, there was a revival of architecture and painting.

54–68, once sent a special expedition to Arabia to ensure that both sides of the Red Sea were in Roman hands.

Because certain products (silk, for example) increased a hundredfold in price by the time they reached their destination, there were great earnings from costly luxury articles. Silk prices were kept high by the Parthians, then by the Sassanian Persian merchants who held a trade monopoly. All attempts to break their cartel were unsuccessful. The Romans in the west had no knowledge of the origin of the silk fabric that was known to them as *serica*, after the Mongolian word for thread. (The Chinese, inventors of silk fabrics, were then called the "Ser" by many, after their luxurious textiles.) At that time silk was thought to be a plant product, like Indian cotton.

The Byzantine emperor Justinian (AD 527–565) was vexed by Sassanian Persian price schemes. He contacted the emperor of Ethiopia and asked him to establish a competitive trade route by way of the East African ports in order to deal Arab traders a considerable economic blow. But the enterprise failed miserably, as the Persians bought as much silk as they could and paid more than the poor Ethiopians offered.

The Persian monopoly would end in a different way. In 552 the emperor received two visitors in the Great Palace of Byzantium. They were monks whom he had sent to China to obtain the eggs of the silkworm and information about silk cultivation. They had returned with the silkworm eggs, which they had smuggled out of China hidden in their hollow canes. Constantinople became the center of the silk trade, retaining that position till the eleventh century.

Religion as an Export

The emissaries of the Indian princes traveled all over the known world to establish new relationships and spread the doctrines of eastern religions. The princes sailed to Java, Sumatra, Bali, and Borneo on their Indian ships, spreading both Hinduism and Buddhism. The Buddhist temple complex of Borobudur on the island of Java is impressive testimony to their evangelical efforts, and on the island of Bali the chief religion is an old form of Brahmanism with traces of the ancient Hindu faith.

The princes also traveled to Cambodia, Burma, and China. From the port city of Tamralipti at the mouth of the Ganges, the ships took on monks along with their icons and manuscripts, as well as cargo. One Chinese scholar and pilgrim by the name of I-tsing, who had undertaken the long journey to India by the Silk Road in 671–695, wrote: "More than a thousand Buddhist monks have applied themselves in the service of scholarship and good works. They investigate and discuss all matters, as they do in India. If a Chinese monk wishes to go to India for study, he might be better off going to the university at Nalanda (in northeast India) or to Taxila (in Pakistan). Only then will he be well prepared to continue his journey in India and to pursue his studies in the country." I-tsing knew what he was talking about. He had spent ten years in Nalanda and translated numerous writings into Chinese.

Science and Mathematics as Exports

Science was also spread from India to the rest of the world. For instance, India used the metric system, which the Arabs called "Indian numerals." The Arabs subsequently introduced these numerals to the West, which in turn called them "Arabic numerals."

Chinese horsemen; painting on silk

The March of Progress

China During the Han Dynasty

Earlier Han Era (206 BC–AD 8)
Liu Pang (First Han Emperor, 256–195 BC)

The collapse of the Chin dynasty in China in 206 BC was partly due to the efforts of a rebellious army officer named Kao Tsu. Leader of one of the many uprisings across China, some of his popularity with the masses may have stemmed from his peasant origins. A bandit before he joined the Chin army, he was a skilled military and political strategist. In 206 BC, having built most of the power base he needed to succeed, he declared himself emperor. Founder of the Han dynasty, he was also called Liu Chi and was posthumously titled Liu Pang.

By 202 BC, he had eliminated virtually all opposition to his authority, either by military

Warrior from
the Han dynasty,
a terra-cotta
statue

means or diplomacy. A pragmatic, effective ruler, he revived the rural economy and lightened the tax burden of the peasants. To reward loyal allies and his own relatives, he granted them hereditary kingdoms. He continued to base his power on the feudal landed nobility.

Both of these practices were altered by his successors. The dynasty he established was noted for its reform. It soon took direct control over virtually all land in its domain, eliminating the kingdoms. The Han emperors introduced a number of innovations rooted in concern for public benefit. Most important, they established Confucianism as the official ideology.

Han Confucianism

The totalitarian practices of the Chin dynasty had been philosophically rooted in legalism, the teaching of Hsün-tzu that people were by nature evil and needed strict laws and punishments to regulate their conduct. Legalism gave rulers unquestioned authority to set up a government with unlimited control over society, even at the expense of individual freedom. The Chin rulers implemented this.

Confucianism, in contrast, looked to the individual as the most important unit in the hierarchy of family, society, and state. Confucius developed his philosophy while advising the rulers of various states in the late 500s and early 400s BC. He sought to reestablish social order through personal right conduct, learned by studying the rules of propriety outlined in the literature of the early Chou dynasty.

The Han Confucians adopted his teachings on the necessary worthiness of and respect for learning, adding to them a legalist emphasis on administration. The Han emperors adopted Confucianism in 136 BC, as well the Confucian principle of appointing officials on the basis of merit. They expanded the bureaucracy to meet the needs of more people. They used the administrative apparatus set by the Chin dynasty but modified many of its policies. They required written examinations to find qualified people, rather than handing out offices on the basis of birth or personal connection. They required the study of Confucianism for government service, establishing a university for bureaucrats in the late second century BC.

They reorganized the system of taxation, generally reducing taxes and establishing uniform levies for the entire empire to take the place of intricate local laws and curren-

Chinese crown
from the seventh
century

1503

cies. They encouraged people to maintain grain reserves against frequently occurring famines.

Emperor Wu Ti (140–87 BC)

Under Emperor Wu Ti, the early Han dynasty reached its peak of expansion. In the west, he fought and negotiated with the Hsiung-nu (possibly related to the Huns), sending forces into the valley of the Jaxartes River (in today's Kazakhstan). His general, Chang Chien, consolidated China's position in the west, forming alliances with

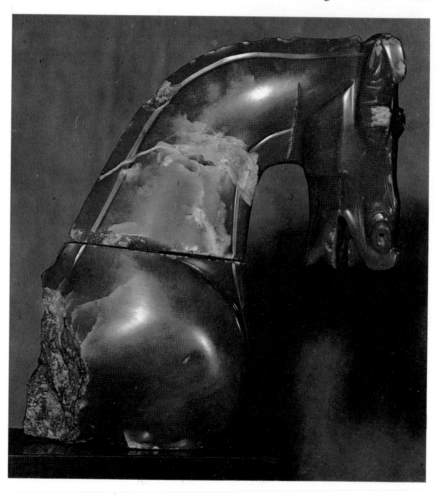

Equestrian head in jade, from the time of the first Han emperors

Samarkand, Bactria, Bokhara, and Ferghana. (The remains of forts and fortifications he built to hold back the Huns can still be found in the Gobi Desert.) China then took the offensive in the north and conquered the Tarim Basin. Wu Ti eventually established imperial control over the southern part of Manchuria and northern Korea. In the south he conquered the island of Hainan. He established colonies in Annam and Korea and ultimately extended Han authority from Korea to Tonkin in Vietnam, although much of the area, especially south of the Chang Jiang, or Ch'ang Chiang (Yangtze), was not completely assimilated. His ambassadors established relations far to the west.

These campaigns required more money

than the emperor had in the imperial treasuries. He (and his successors) raised taxes, restored the practice of government monopolies that had been abolished by earlier Han emperors, and debased the currency. Even the lucrative Silk Road, the great trade route once made secure by the military operations of Chang Chien, was discontinued. Not until 87 BC would caravans again undertake the long journey to China.

Popular Discontent

Things got worse under Wu Ti's successors. Imperial authority declined. Babies frequently inherited the throne, leaving the once-competent government administration at the mercy of regent-mothers who appointed relatives at will, regardless of qualification. This fostered intrigue and partisanship.

The financial situation deteriorated as provincial landholding families refused to pay taxes and were given tax-exempt status. The government still needed the funds and so passed the burden on to the peasants by raising taxes. Individual farmers were already having trouble, forced to split up their lands as the population grew. Some turned to banditry, others to rebellion.

Hsin Dynasty (8–23 AD)

Wang Mang, the founder of the short-lived Hsin dynasty, is known as "the Usurper." His father's half sister was empress of the Han dynasty in China. In 16 BC Wang Mang was given a noble title and later appointed to a regency. He outmaneuvered his opponents and had his daughter enthroned as empress under a fourteen-year-old emperor, P'ing, who died suddenly. Wang Mang was accused of the murder by his enemies. He solved the succession problem by selecting from among the eligible heirs a one-year-old boy who was not officially enthroned but called the Young Prince, while Wang Mang was given the title of acting emperor.

He easily subdued his opponents and propagandized that Heaven was calling for the end to the Han dynasty and that he had the mandate for a new one. On January 10, AD 9, Wang Mang ascended the throne and proclaimed the foundation of the Hsin dynasty.

Wang Mang was a Confucian, a politician, and a teacher who followed the agrarian and monetary policies of the Han dynasty. He was also a legal hard-liner who had three of his sons executed, along with a grandson and a nephew. On the other hand, he supported scholarship and led China successfully in its foreign policy.

It was a natural catastrophe that ended his dynasty: between AD 2 and 5, and also in AD 11, the Yellow River changed its course,

Figurine of a camel driver, found in a tomb of the Hue period.

devastating a large populated area. Famine and epidemics led to civil war and migration. One of the rebellious peasant groups, known as the Red Eyebrows, defeated Wang Mang's armies and other rebellions ensued. The palace was set afire, and several days later, on October 6, AD 23, Wang Mang and his followers were assassinated.

Later Han Era (25–220 AD)
The problem of infant emperors and incompetent regent-mothers reappeared to add to the general administrative disarray in the later Han dynasty. Emperors enlisted the help of court eunuchs, or castrated men (a commonly accepted social phenomenon), only to create a demand on their part for influence. Factional struggles led to battle.

The Han dynasty had other problems, as well. The great landowners established local autonomy with their own private armies. In

Woman on horseback: figurine from the Tang period

1505

Model of a
watch tower, exhumed
from a grave of the
Han dynasty.

184 Taoist societies organized rebellions that lasted for decades. The Yellow Turbans devastated Shandong until 204. In Sichuan (Szechwan) the Five Pecks of Rice Society continued its wars until Han general Ts'ao Ts'ao halted them in 215. His son took the throne in 220, establishing the Wei dynasty.

Despite its conflicts, the long era of the Hans had seen major developments. In the period of peace provided by Wu Ti, Ssu-ma Chien (145–97 BC) wrote his important *Chronicles of a Historian*, a pattern for subsequent generations of Chinese historians. Trade increased along the "Silk Road," the caravan route at last made safe. Chinese silk even reached a distant place the Chinese called *Ta-tsi Tsin*. (Its inhabitants called it Imperium Romanum.) The water clock and the sundial were invented. In AD 105 Tsai-Lun made the first paper from rags and plant fiber.

The Six Dynasties (220–581)

The time of China's fragmentation into several dynastic realms and some sixteen non-Chinese kingdoms is called the Six Dynasties period. Rival dynasties to the Wei Kingdom, both also related to the Han dynasty, were established: the Shu (221–263) in southwestern China and the Wu (222–280) in the Chang Jiang (Yangtze) Valley to the southeast, with Nanking as its capital. The Three Kingdoms waged incessant and inconclusive warfare between 220 and 265 (the era named for them). In 265 the

Terra-cotta
statuette of a dancer,
a grave gift from
the Han period

1507

Wei general Ssu-ma Yen seized that throne, establishing the Chin dynasty (265–317) and reuniting north and south by 280. The dynasty remained stable until his death in 290.

Non-Chinese tribes started to invade from the north in 304. By 317 they had taken control of north China from the Chin dynasty. They would keep it for almost three centuries, setting up sixteen separate realms not accorded dynastic names. In the south four Chinese dynasties ruled in turn.

The rest of society became feudal. Large landowners ran self-sufficient manors farmed by peasants who traded work for protection and became dependents. Most

Silver-plated chalice from the Han period

manors were well fortified and guarded by private armies.

The Sui Dynasty (581–618)
In 581 a servant in military service named Yang Chien seized possession of the throne of the non-Chinese northern Chou. He had himself proclaimed emperor, establishing the Sui dynasty, and proceeded to conquer south China. He unified China after a long period of discord. He revived and centralized the administrative system the Han dynasty had established, including the competitive examinations for bureaucrats (or mandarins). He made Confucianism the state ideology but welcomed the contributions of Taoism and Buddhism.

Over his short reign he accomplished a great deal. He dug a canal (later part of the thousand-mile-, or 1,609-kilometer-, long

Grand Canal) to carry the farm produce of the Chang Jiang (Yangtze) delta to the north. He repaired the Great Wall and built a series of splendid palaces and Buddhist temples in his new capital of Changan. He had the country's administration completely overhauled and its criminal law adjusted to current conditions. He reclaimed northern Vietnam, but his efforts in Manchuria and Korea were unsuccessful. Li Yuan deposed him in 617.

The Tang Dynasty (618–907)
The Tang dynasty founded by Li Yuan produced a genuine reformation of government, including a reorganization of the civil service that lasted into the twentieth century. The emperor rewrote the government entry examination and founded the Han-li Academy for history. He centralized the administration and developed a code of administrative and penal law. Under the first Tang emperor, Kao-tsu, China was probably the largest empire in the world. Its generals occupied parts of Turkestan, Korea, Pamir, and Tibet. Through treaties with tribes in Central Asia, it dominated the Tarim Basin. Tang influence was evident in Japan, southern Manchuria, and northern Vietnam.

Foreign trade expanded over the caravan routes and over the seas through the port of Guangzhou. One great emperor followed another and the country prospered as never before. This prosperity was reflected in art and literature. In the early Tang era, the capital, Changan, was renowned for its culture and religious toleration. Buddhism reached its peak of popularity.

Tang political decline began in the eighth century as literature flourished. Over a thousand major poets are known from this period. Printing was discovered, using loose wooden letters, which permitted large-scale production of texts. Later emperors published a newsletter for their officials throughout the country. The Tangs used the new invention to print the first paper money.

The Tang had a system of taxation based on land allotments for adult males. The dynasty drew its military from the same men, requiring periodic militia service. Problems arose as taxes per capita remained the same and population growth led to the inheritance of much smaller parcels of land. Peasant resentment was increased by the fact that tax-free estates were still granted to the favored. Peasants who could not pay the taxes on their allotments ran away. This deprived the government of revenue and the military of soldiers. The problem was so bad that a system of commanderies, which entailed hiring non-Chinese mercenaries for

Illustration depicting the Mandarin examinations in ancient China

the border militia, was created. In 751 they were blamed for the defeat by the Talas that cost the Tang the Tarim area.

Buddhism
Buddhism had spread to China from India. Given the population density involved, half the world was Buddhist by the fourth century. Much of northern China was then converted and, by AD 600, most of the country. As Confucianism became equated with maintenance of the status quo and corrupt officials, the appeal of Buddhism, with its emphasis on morality, detachment from earthly things, and inner tranquility, grew.

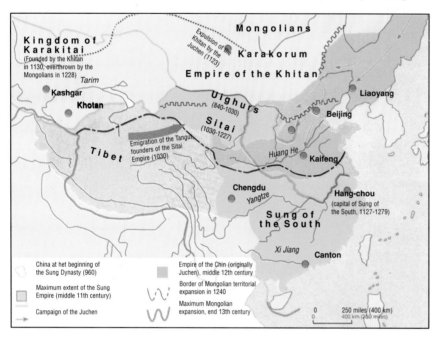

China during
the Sung dynasty,
960–1279

Taoism, with its emphasis on individual harmony with the Way of Nature (Tao), not to be interfered with by government, gained great popularity at the same time.

The toleration of the early Tang for both religions gave way to a marked revival of Confucianism, particularly among the growing class of officials, by the late Tang era. Buddhism began to be regarded as a disruption of the social order, not to be condoned by the state religion, Confucianism. Although religious toleration was largely practiced, foreign cultures were sometimes proscribed, and on several occasions Buddhist monasteries were dissolved, at great profit to the state treasuries.

Five Dynasties Period (907–960)
The Tang dynasty was still nominally in power until the last emperor was deposed in 907. Once again China experienced a period of disunion. Five short-lived dynasties followed in sequence in the Huang He Valley. Ten independent kingdoms were established at about the same time, most in south China.

The Khitan Mongol Liao dynasty (907–1125) expanded from Manchuria and Mongolia to parts of northern China (Hebei and Shanxi) and made Beijing the southern capital of a Sino-Khitan empire.

The Northern Sung Dynasty (960–1126)
This division continued until 960, when General Chao K'uang-yin seized the throne and declared himself emperor of the Sung dynasty (960–1279). (It is considered separately as northern and southern Sung.) By 978 he had reconquered most of China, excluding only the areas held by the Liao dynasty. He made his capital at Kaifeng.

With the increased trade opportunities fostered by peace, Chao K'uang-yin brought back prosperity. Towns expanded and new institutions began to function: fire departments, municipal police, orphanages, hospitals, public baths, welfare agencies, even an agricultural testing station. The Sung emperors subordinated the army to the civil service and expanded its examination to admit applicants outside the nobility. Education, the arts and literature, philosophy, engineering, astronomy, and mathematics flourished. Women were allowed to participate, resulting in the rise of several female poets and painters and an archaeologist.

The military, however, was weak. After frequent defeats the Sung signed a treaty with the Liao in 1004, giving them the land they already seized in the north and agreeing to annual tribute. In 1044 the Sung agreed to pay tribute to the Hsi Hsia, a Tangut tribe on the northwest border.

Tribute was costly, as were military operations and the large bureaucracy. The economy was unable to keep up with burgeoning population growth. There was bitter rivalry over various proposals for reform. To survive, the Sung allied with the Chin dynasty (1122–1234) of northern Manchuria against the Liao some time in the 1120s. Together they defeated the Liao in 1125. The Chin moved on against the Sung, seizing Kaifeng in 1126.

The Southern Sung (1127–1279)
The loss of Kaifeng marks the start of the southern Sung era. The Sung retreated to Hangzhou, making it their capital in 1135. The dynasty controlled only south China, but its economic and intellectual accomplishments outstripped those of the conquered northern Sung. It showed little sign of any insurmountable problems when it was faced with a new threat, the Mongols.

The Mongols
It was about 1200 when Chingiz (Genghis)

Khan led the first Mongol horsemen over the Great Wall that formed the southern border of his tribal father's domain. Inheriting the leadership of a loose confederation of Mongol nomadic sheepherding tribes, he built an intensely loyal and disciplined fighting force. It was characterized by superb horsemanship and archery, extraordinary mobility, and astonishing cruelty. The khan had established his own code of right and wrong, basing it on a concept of equality among the Mongols that overrode their former intertribal rivalry. His interest was seasonal plunder rather than systematic conquest. For years, the hordes (a Mongol horde was a unit of ten thousand soldiers) entered China in the summer to pillage and returned to the Mongolian steppes in winter. The display of power, wanton or not, had its effect. Impressed generals and high officials defected, providing the illiterate Mongols with the services of people who could read and write and who were familiar with technologies

Chao K'uang-yin, first emperor of the Sung dynasty

Chinese piece
of ceramic work, dating
from the seventh
century

Statuette from the
Han period, made of
varnished clay
and depicting the
god of death

unknown to them. In 1213 Chingiz (Genghis) Khan led his armies to the Shantung Peninsula. In 1215 he razed Beijing, extending his control over the Chin dynasty in northern China. He died in 1227. His grandsons Mangu and Kublai Khan, seizing almost all of China, completed the conquest he had begun.

Kublai Khan established his capital, Khan-balik (Cambaluc), near Beijing in 1264, making it an international center of great renown. He conquered the Southern Sung in 1279, after he had succeeded to Mongol leadership. Although the rest of China was already in Mongol hands, the Chinese fleet at sea tried to defend both empire and emperor. It suffered overwhelming defeat. The admiral drowned, holding in his arms the infant who was the last of the Sung emperors.

Kublai Khan established the Mongol Yüan dynasty the same year, becoming its first emperor. He and his successors ruled under the dynastic title Yüan. Although he was a committed Buddhist and made Buddhism the state religion, he permitted the practice of other religions. He adopted the bureaucratic system of the Chinese but excluded Chinese from positions of authority, replacing them with Mongols. After his death in 1294, the Mongols chose his grandson Timur as successor. The dynasty continued in the face of growing resentment at all levels of society.

Mongol rule fomented discord among the Chinese, regardless. Chinese officials, primarily Confucians, objected to their reduced status. Peasants objected to new taxes. The crop failures, resultant famine, and inflation combined with Huang He floods led to widespread civil discontent and provincial rebellion in the 1330s and 1340s. By the 1360s a former Buddhist monk named Chu Yuanchang gained control of the Yangtze Valley.

The ninth khan after Kublai was deposed after an uprising. In 1368 the native Ming dynasty came to power with Nanking as its capital.

Fresco in the Sophia Church in Kyyiv (Kiev); this church was built in the eleventh century during the reign of Yaroslav, son of Vladimir.

From Kiev to Moscow

The First Russian Kingdoms

Slavic tribes, hunters and traders, migrated to the vast plains between the Black Sea and the Arctic sometime before the fourth century AD to settle the area that would become Russia. They used the rivers spawned by the Valdayskaya Hills northeast of the Carpathian Mountains to transport goods between the Baltic and the Black Seas. They set up trading posts on the rivers: Novgorod, on the Volkhov, and Kyyiv (modern Kiev), which was firmly established as the major city of Rus in the middle of the sixth century, on the Dnepr. Scandinavian traders based on the

northern lakes Ladoga and Onega established an outpost at Ryazan on the Oka River.

Islamic and Western sources mention a *Rus Khagan* (prince of princes) on the Volga River about AD 830, who ruled over the allied eastern tribes. The name *Russia* stems from the name of the river *Rus*.

In the eighth and early ninth centuries the Rus people traded with the caliphate of Baghdad as well as the Byzantine capital of Constantinople. Their fleets were a major presence on the Black Sea. In 860 they attacked Constantinople. Meanwhile, rival

1513

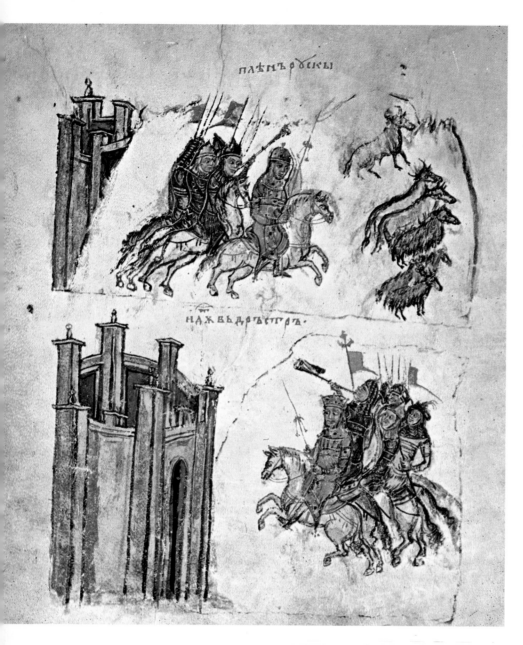

Two drawings
showing the Russian prince
Svyatoslav going
to battle

dynastic clans of Scandinavians (called *Varangians*) raided and traded their way down the rivers, led by their princes. One of these princes was Rurik.

The House of Rurik

The loosely united Slavic tribes that formed the territory of Rus until the middle of the ninth century did not have a fixed capital or common leader. Around 860, however, the Varangian prince Rurik rose to power in Novgorod and united the tribes of northern Rus under him. He is seen as the progenitor of the dynasty that would dominate much of the East Slavic territory until 1598. Rurik, regarded by many historians as the founder of the Russian Empire, ushered in a period of Slavic expansion in which Slavs migrated north, replacing or assimilating the native Finnics.

Oleg and Igor

Rurik's son Igor, a child, succeeded him in 879. In 882, the regent, Prince Oleg, a relation of Rurik, ordered the assassination of the Varangian rulers of Kyyiv, which he merged with Novgorod. He made Kyyiv the capital of the first significant Russian state, called Kievan Rus, and signed a trade treaty with the Byzantine Empire. Igor, assuming power from Oleg the next year, ruled for over three decades, gaining territory. He died in 945. His widow, Olga, succeeded him and converted to Christianity. Olga was responsible for organizing the territories into a coherent governmental structure and for expanding the influence of the princes of Kyyiv.

Svyatoslav

In 964 the queen abdicated in favor of her son Svyatoslav, who rejected his mother's Christianity, since it would make him a subject of the Byzantine Empire.

He developed the East Slavic kingdom into a large empire in the Ukraine by the end of the tenth century. Svyatoslav was ambushed by the nomadic Petchenegs in 972 at the bidding of Byzantine rulers. His sons fought for the throne until 980, when the youngest son, Vladimir, took it.

Vladimir the Great (reigned 980–1015)

Vladimir the Great (Vladimir I), architect of the Kievan state, established a seniority system for his own clan, promulgated his

Fourteenth century
Russian fresco depicting
two Christian martyrs

realm's code of law, and converted it to Byzantine Christianity.

Initially a pagan, Vladimir was far more concerned with the obliteration of opposition and the pursuit of his own pleasures than with religion. His focus remained the consolidation of his empire until 988. After joining with Vladimir in the suppression of a rebellion, Byzantine Emperor Basil II invited him to marry his sister Anne. After marrying Anne and accepting Christianity, he outlawed paganism and made Christianity the official religion. The Orthodox Church conferred posthumous sainthood on him.

Yaroslav the Wise (reigned 1019–1054)

Vladimir died in 1015, setting off a series of family assassinations. The eldest son, Svyatopolk the Accursed, was accorded highest authority in 1015. This caused resentment from his brothers Boris and Gleb, whom Svyatopolk had killed. He was then deposed by another brother, Yaroslav, prince of Novgorod, in 1019.

By 1036, Yaroslav the Wise created a great Russian empire, stretching from the Black Sea to the Gulf of Finland. He developed a system of inheritance by precedence to avoid the internecine rivalry following the death of the grand duke of Kyyiv.

The Decline of Kyyiv

Yaroslav's system was only nominally followed after his death in 1054. Most of Vladimir's innumerable grandsons inherited lands and acquired interests in conflict with each other and imperial unity. A profusion of warring city-states developed, most still ruled by vying relatives of the House of Rurik.

Turkic nomads involved themselves in the disputes, often taking opposite sides. In 1097 members of the dynasty and Turkic allies

Prince Jaropolk and his wife at St Peter's feet. With the death of this prince Kyyiv definitively lost its unity. 1515

divided up the whole Kievan Rus. Vladimir II Monomachus, grandson of Yaroslav, tried to reunite it, but the decline continued.

Trade, too, was a factor undermining Kyyiv, which had lost its major trading partner, Constantinople, when the Crusaders sacked it in 1204. Many people left Kyyiv for Novgorod. (The Hanseatic League, a federation of German cities controlling the Baltic trade, used Novgorod as a base in the

Fifteenth century fresco depicting the deposition of Christ.

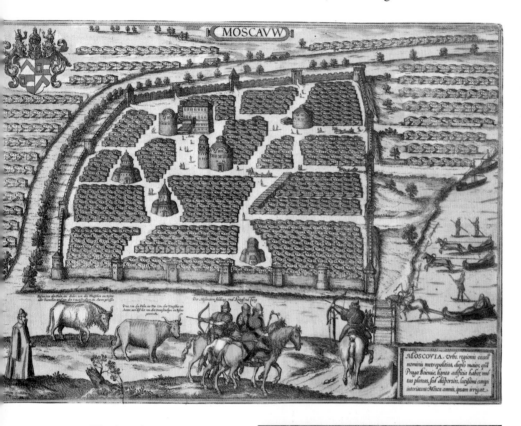

The Austrian envoy Sigismund von Herberstein visited Moscow in 1517 and 1526.
Around 1547 he made a woodcut "View of Moscow" which is not very reliable. After Herberstein had used the woodcut as an illustration in his not very complimentary travel book on Moscow and the Kremlin (Basel 1556) the picture was very successful and was adopted by other cartographers such as Johannes Janssonius in Amsterdam.

Russian icon from the fifteenth century, depicting Jesus Christ.

thirteenth century.) Galicia and Volhynia in the west, Suzdal, Polatsk, Smolensk, Chernigov, and Novgorod-Severski were rivals.

Central authority was also challenged by the *boyars*, the high ranking nobility. Border incursions were yet another threat, but the greatest danger was from Mongols.

Mongols

Mongol hordes first appeared in the southeast in 1223, menacing the Polovtzy, who sent for Russian aid against this common enemy. Yet after their victory over an allied army on the Kalka River, the Mongols were recalled by the khan. They did not return until 1237, when Batu Khan, grandson of Chingiz (Genghis) Khan, led his Golden Horde on a rampage through the major cities in the Vladimir-Suzdal region. He sacked Kyyiv in 1240. Prince Alexander Nevsky saved Novgorod only by paying ransom. Batu made Sarai (on the lower Volga) the capital of his khanate of Kipchak in 1242. and exacted tributes from the Russian cities under this domination. Tribute payment would continue into the fifteenth century.

The Mongols held sway in southern Russia until the late fifteenth century. Novgorod and the Russian principalities were dependencies of the khanate.

The grand duke of Moscow, Dmitry

Power in the Empire of Kyyiv

The political history of Kyyiv (Kiev) starts with Oleg's legendary conquest of the town on the Dnepr River in 882. It is unclear exactly when the empire ceased to exist. According to some historians the end of the empire coincided with the death of Yaroslav the Wise. Others are of the opinion that Vladimir Monomakh—who reigned from 1113 until 1125—was the last ruler. The same is said of Mstislav, who was in power from 1125 until 1132. A third group of historians see the conquest of Kyyiv in 1169 by Prince Andrew Bogolyubsky as the end of the empire that was once so powerful. But there is a good case for sticking to the date of 1240. It was in this year that Kyyiv was completely destroyed by the Mongols. This was the beginning of the Mongol domination of Russia, which was to last two hundred years. The most important political institutions of the Kyyiv Empire were the office of prince, the *duma* (the council of boyars), and the *veche*, or city council. The prince of Kyyiv held a special position. From the twelfth century onward he was called "the grand prince." Not only was he in command of the soldiers, his duties also included jurisdiction and government. When war broke out, the prince could first rely on his own liegemen, the so-called *druzhina*. In addition, he could always make an appeal to regiments of major towns, and as a last resort there was the possibility of a general mobilization. The military history of Kyyiv was a very rich one. The Russia of later years was to benefit greatly from the organization and military experience of the armies of Kyyiv. The judicial system of Kyyiv shows that society in those days was very well organized, especially as far as trade and finance were concerned. The lenient punishments are striking, too. The punishment for breaking the law was not the death penalty, but a fine, which can be considered fairly revolutionary. In addition to taxes on fireplaces and ploughshares, the princes also collected money by levying fines and taxes on trade. On the face of it the boyar duma, which included senior clergymen, seems similar to a parliament. It was, however, quite different. The prince's power was not really curtailed by the duma. The boyar duma was an important institution, however, since the boyars worked in close cooperation with the prince and advised him constantly. The veche, or city council, on the other hand, had democratic characteristics. All male heads of family were entitled to participate in its sessions, which were generally held in the marketplace. The veche made decisions in matters such as war and peace, emergency legislation, and conflicts with the prince or between princes themselves. As decisions had to be reached by unanimity of votes, one might speak of a form of direct democracy. In Kyyiv, especially, the veche played an important role. But there were also veches elsewhere in Russia. Even in Novgorod there was to be a veche, later in history.

Trade route in the Empire of Kyyiv.

Donskoy ("of the Don"), won a significant victory over the Golden Horde in 1380. The battle at Kukikovo on the Don River marked the rise of Muscovite power. A hundred years later, Ivan III Vasilyevich finally abolished the payment of tribute to the Mongols.

While Kievan civilization declined under Mongol rule, Moscow grew in importance. It assumed a new leadership role, rivaled only by the Polish-Lithuanian Empire the Latin Christians had carved out of western Kievan Rus.

Muscovy

Daniel, progenitor of the dukes of Moscow, or Muscovy, had received the town from his father, Alexander Nevsky, in 1263. Daniel established a dynasty in Moscow that would eventually become the sovereign power of Russia. His son Ivan I took over in 1328. He was permitted by the Mongols to annex territory to Moscow.

After the fall of Constantinople to the Osman Turks in 1453, church and dukes alike regarded Moscow as the "third Rome." Self-titled czar (Slavic for caesar or emperor), Ivan III annexed Novgorod in 1478 and Tver in 1485, the same year he ended Mongol tribute. He had seized much of the Polish-Lithuanian kingdom by 1503.

Ivan the Terrible (reigned 1533–1584)

Ivan IV Vasilyevich, called the Terrible for his cruelty, inherited Moscow when he was three years old. His mother ruled in relative calm until her death in 1538. Under unstable circumstances Ivan took power in 1547 as the first czar and wedded Anastasia Romanovna the same year. Shortly after he was crowned, the city of Moscow was devastated by fire. The disgruntled populace blamed the czar and his family, and rebellion broke out in the city. After punishing the rebels, Ivan created a new assembly in 1549 to broaden social representation. He announced his abdication in 1564 as a successful ruse to get absolute power, thereby setting the pattern for czarist supremacy.

He used his private military force to suppress, torture, and murder boyar opponents. By 1581 his armies had opened Siberia to Russia.

From the mid-1560s until his death, Ivan IV repressed his opponents with brutality.

Between 1485 and 1508 a new rampart was built around the Kremlin, where Czar Ivan the Great's court and seat of government were. This brick wall with its characteristic battlements are still to be seen. The new fortifications were built by the Italians Marco Ruffo and Petro Solario after the example of the impressive Sforza fortress in Milan. The wall is 7,333 feet (2,235 metres) long and 16 to 30 feet (5 to 9 meters) high. The width varies between 11 and 20 feet (3.5 and 6 metres). It has 15 square and 3 round protruding towers, only four of which are fitted with gates. The impressive superstructure dates from the seventeenth century whereas the stars which adorn it are from the twentieth century. The height of the towers varies between 89 and 262 feet (27 and 80 metres).
View of the court with the Nicholas Tower and the Senate Tower.

1518

Fifteenth century Russian cross, embellished with pearls

Todai Temple in Nara, built around 747 by a prince of the Taika clan

The Emergence of Japan

A Civilization Emerges on the
Border of the Chinese Cultural Sphere

It is a commonly held belief that Japan and mainland Asia were connected during the Pleistocene Age. The origins of the Japanese people and the earliest forms of their society are not known with certainty, but they probably trace to the hunting and gathering cultures of Asia's temperate forests. The art of writing was imported from China fairly late, which is why there are no historical sources from this period. Since the 1960s, excavation archaeology has become an area of intense study in Japan, with interesting results.

The Japanese archipelago made a stable foraging existence possible. Recent Paleolithic evidence dates the earliest human settlement in Japan to possibly 200,000

Granite statue of izo-sama, the god who protects children; from the island of Sado

Fertility goddess from the Jōmon culture; from the island of Hinshu

were ethnically diverse, from Northeast and Southeast Asia. They were hunter-gatherers and fishermen but did not yet engage actively in agriculture, although there is evidence that they were knowledgeable horticulturalists who collected and stored wild plants. Dogs were their only domesticated animals. The Jōmon lived in semisubterranean pit houses with thatched roofs that were supported by posts. They also built large ceremonial structures and storage pits. Their pottery demonstrates superior quality and craftsmanship, and they also made lacquered vessels and elaborate wood carvings.

The second culture is called the Yayoi, after a neighborhood in Tokyo where the first artifacts were found in 1884. The Yayoi culture flourished from 400 BC to AD 250. It apparently originated from rice-cultivating peoples migrating from China by way of the Ryūjyū Islands and the Korean Peninsula to the southern island of Kyūshū. The people were familiar with agriculture, in particular irrigated rice cultivation, and used methods that were customary on the Asian mainland during this same period. Local populations adapted these innovations. Thanks to highly developed rice cultivation, the population must have grown considerably during the Yayoi period. The Yayoi utilized numerous tools of polished stone, metal weapons and mirrors, and manufactured pottery. It was also at that time that pigs were domesticated and chickens kept as sacred birds.

During this entire period, and up into historical times, there was a continuous influx of new people into the Japanese archipelago. Some of this migration was connected to the Warring States period in China. The migrants would arrive from the Korean Peninsula, which for thousands of years served as the bridge across which new ideas and new people traveled into Japan. During that period the Chin and Han emperors ruled China and protected its borders so well that any immigrants were forced to traverse the remote areas of Korea.

Both bronze and iron were known during this era, the bronze being used chiefly for ceremonial purposes. The Yayoi peoples also made glass.

The Tomb Culture

Around AD 250 the Tomb culture emerged, with the Kinai region on Japan's Inland Sea as its major center. Testimony to the emergence of great chiefs in western Japan are the gigantic burial mounds in areas around Osaka and in present-day Gumma, Kyūshū, and Okayama. The Kofun peoples buried their rulers under mounds of soil and stones, along with objects symbolic of military

years ago, with tools the earliest evidence. Human fossils have been found in Okinawa that are 10,000 to 30,000 years old, and lithic finds give some indication of the patterns of settlements. Waste dumps have been found containing the shells of the mollusks the first Japanese ate, as well as other food remains. In addition, archaeologists have found remains of huts and pottery, which led them to conclude there had been two major Neolithic cultures in Japan: the Jōmon and Yayoi cultures.

Between 10,500 and 400 BC, the Jōmon culture was dominant. Finds from that civilization have been made all over Japan. To a certain degree, these resemble the remains found in Eastern Siberia that, according to some scholars, is where the early Japanese people came from. For a long time, the Ainu, a people living in northern Japan, were considered the descendants of the Jōmon. This theory was recently discarded. The Jōmon

An eighth century
Japanese empress and her
prime minister

power and social control: special funerary ceramics, weapons, and horse gear. In the late sixth century this particular burial method was abandoned as no longer appropriate according to the tenets of the Buddhism that took hold in Japan earlier that century.

Overseas trade was a major activity in the Kofun period. Archaeologists found objects in graves similar to those they had encountered in Manchuria and Korea, such as the *magatama* (meaning "bent jewelry"), an ornament that, combined with the bronze mirror and the iron sword two centuries later, would become the emperor's insignia, symbolizing the subordination of local chiefs to a central ruler. Kofun-style tombs were also guarded by *haniwa,* cylindrical hollow clay statues found on the burial mounds depicting men, women, animals, birds, fish, and houses.

Inscribed iron swords preserve the records of political relationships in the fifth century. We also rely on interpretations of the *Kojiki,* an epic written in the seventh century

Statuette of a Japanese god

1522

describing the creation of the world and showing the emperor to be the legitimate inheritor of power. The latter section describes the story of Emperor Jimmu, the Divine Warrior who departed from Kyūshū in 660 BC to establish his rule on the remaining islands. He is traditionally considered Japan's first emperor who, on the first day of spring, founded the state of Japan on the Yamato plain. Such a person as Jimmu must indeed have existed, though modern historians would rather place him in the third or fourth century AD.

The precise founding date of the state of Japan cannot be determined. Not until the early fifth century did archaeological data, Chinese chronicles, and Japanese sources combine to create one consistent picture of Japanese history. At the end of the sixth century, historical chronicles became more reliable.

The Men of the Sun Line, the Uji System
The emperor had a sacred function. During the early period the entire population of Japan professed a belief in an amalgam of local cults and philosophies based on ancestor worship. The foremost deity, however, was the sun goddess Amaterasu. The emperor was her most important priest and also her mythological descendant, the reason for which the rising sun was used later as a symbol of Japan.

The Japan that slowly emerges from this historical light was divided into *uji,* clans or lineage groups that were a result of diplomacy, clan warfare, and conquest, not of religious belief per se. The emperor, who also performed a priestly function, was the head of all clans. Each subordinate clan had its own god, which of course was in a lower category than the sun goddess. At the emperor's court the clan chieftains were often involved in political disputes and violence. Aside from the clans, the Japanese also formed *be,* or communities of workers. Before the seventh century these brotherhoods were tied to a form of craftsmen's guilds, the so-called *be.* Makers of weaponry in particular took on great authority in war-oriented Japan.

Buddha (daibutsu) from the Nara period; this statue is in the hall of the Todaiji Temple.

Shi-tenno,
a heavenly king; from
Toshodaiji, Nara

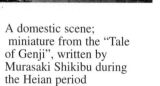

A domestic scene;
miniature from the "Tale
of Genji", written by
Murasaki Shikibu during
the Heian period

1524

Originally, the Yamato Empire probably consisted of a cluster of uji ruled by the dominant uji of the Sun Line, who claimed descent from the sun goddess. In the fifth century the Sun Line clan had established a vague dominance over other uji principalities.

By the sixth century there was a set of rank titles and a council of state. For the emperor it was often difficult to maintain his authority toward his personal clan. He attempted this by placing the other uji in a hierarchy based on relationship to the royal line. True centralization of power came after *Taika* (the Great Change) reform in 645.

Chinese and Korean Influences
At the end of the sixth century, in 587, the Soga clan dominated the country's government after being victorious in a war of succession. The religious consequence of this victory was the rise of Buddhism championed by the Soga, who were relative newcomers, at the expense of clan-centered religion. Buddhism marked the high point of innovations introduced from Chinese and Korean influences, such as script, political doctrine, the practice of Confucianism, the art and theory of Buddhism, technological innovations, and the art and philosophy of a highly civilized society. But Buddhism also challenged the political order that was based on descent from ancestral deities.

Umako (?–626), the Soga leader, had the emperor, his nephew, assassinated in 592, empowering the Soga, who were in control of succession but not of the throne itself. Empress Suiko, Umako's niece, was succeeded by her nephew, Shōtoku Taishi (574–622). As a great admirer of China, he tried to support the Yamato sovereign and the creation of an imperial state by installing a type of Chinese hierarchy. In 603 he created a series of twelve ranks, and in 604 a code of government. Shōtoku promoted Buddhism by writing commentary on the religious writings that had come to Japan from China. During his reign of thirty years Shōtoku had been much admired. But his death and the death soon after of Soga no Umako initiated another period of bitter rivalry.

Chinese Administration; Taika Reforms
A coalition of families led by an imperial prince resisted Soga power by availing themselves of Chinese advisers and Japanese who had returned from study in T'ang China. Several attempts were made to unseat the Soga, but it was not until 645 that the reformers gained the upper hand. During the palace revolution known as the Taika coup d'etat, the Soga leader was assassinated, and the reform coalition began a reorganization of the political order. Emperor Kotoku demanded absolute rule. In 646 the nobles realized the result: no one was allowed to own land or people, the *be* were abolished, and peasants became free leaseholders of the state.

In 702 the centralized Chinese system was fully introduced with some adaptations for Japanese political realities. Lineage remained politically important. The system operat-

Tamamushi shrine
from the Horyu Ji Temple,
depicting the story
of Buddha in a previous
incarnation,
c. AD 650

1525

Carved wooden
statue of Jizo (Japanese god)
of the Heian period,
eleventh century
AD

ed reasonably well in places where the court
had actual influence.

A Series of Capitals

Japan had no established capital city before
the eighth century. The court traveled from
one residence to the other, perhaps out of fear
that the emperor might die in his capital,
which was considered a defilement. Empress
Gemmyo was the first Japanese monarch to
found a capital. In 710 construction was
begun, using the Chinese Tang dynasty capital of Chang-an as a model. The city was to
measure 3 miles by 2.5 miles (4.8 kilometers
by 4 kilometers), but only one quarter of it
was ever completed.

Judging from the existing ruins, the city
must have been very impressive. Anyone of
any importance made sure to live in the new
center, Nara, officially known as Heijō.

Nara must have been a splendid capital.
Unfortunately, the city lost its political significance rather quickly. In 794 Emperor
Kammu (reigned 781–806), a strong ruler
who curbed the power of the local leaders
and the Buddhists, moved to the site where
Heian-Kyo, or Kyoto, the "capital of peace
and tranquillity," was being developed under
his leadership.

The Fujiwara Period (858–1160)

As the Japanese Empire evolved, the population was continually forced to find more
arable land. This search caused conflicts
with the Ezo, who suffered from these
migrations. The emperor, forced to maintain
a large standing army to ward off the wrath
of this tribe, instituted a general draft. Every
third man between the ages of 20 and 60 had
to serve. His family was responsible for supplying him with weapons and provisions.
Military service lasted four years. Obligatory
conscription—abandoned in 792 in favor of
local militia—placed a great burden on the
family of the soldiers.

From the ninth to the twelfth centuries an
aristocracy controlled by the Fujiwara family dominated Japan. Presenting themselves
as an ancient uyi, the Fujiwara family penetrated the government on all levels.
Whenever the Fujiwara considered the
emperor incompetent to rule, they would
request he abdicate. The emperor would
often be happy to oblige. The prospect of a
calm and prosperous retirement was often
very tempting. The Fujiwara preferred to
occupy two posts, *sessho* (regent to a minor)
and *kampaku* (regent to an adult). The two
offices combined meant a powerful hold
over the throne. In 858 the head of the
Fujiwara clan put his seven-year-old grandson on the royal throne as regent.

View on the Japanese volcano Fuji

Culturally speaking, the Fujiwara period was the great classical age of Japanese art and literature, during which predominant Chinese elements were refined by Japanese tastes and innovations to create a unique Japanese culture. In the ninth century the art of writing was greatly diminished and Chinese influence lessened by the invention of the *kana* system of phonetic syllables. In 905 the *Kokin-shu*, more than a thousand poems on many topics divided into twenty books, was compiled, setting the standard for Japanese poetry for centuries. Great classical diaries, most written by women, and the first major novel written in any language, *The Tale of Genji*, also by a woman, were watershed creations setting this period apart.

Toward the end of this period, the capital began to decline. The court and its courtiers began to lose power. No taxes were collected, and the coffers of the royal treasury were

Part of the imperial palace in Kyoto

1527

Torii in the harbor of Itsuku-shima, built around 1170. A torii is a gateway to a Shinto shrine.

Japanese drawing from the twelfth century, depicting an eye operation

pay the upkeep. There were attempts at reform during the eleventh century, such as Emperor Go-Sanjo's unsuccessful attempt in 1068 to confiscate large estates without the authority of the Fujiwara. But even the Fujiwara were unable to escape impoverishment, and by 1110 they were definitively eliminated as a political factor.

Civil War, the Samurai

In the twelfth century the *samurai,* the knights of feudal Japan, assumed power, though officially the emperor retained authority. The samurai were provincial warriors who resembled medieval European knights and who managed the estates of aristocrats, sometimes holding land themselves.

The Heiji War (1159–60) was fueled by rivalry between the Taira and the Minamo, two warrior clans, over court succession. The Taira, who were victorious, became the power behind the imperial throne for twenty years. In a revolt begun in 1180 the Taira's position of power was challenged by the Minamoto family, who deprived the ruling family of its position through a number of intensely fought battles.

The Kamakura Period, the Shogunate

Yoritomo Minamoto (1147–1199) brought the Minamoto family victory in 1185 and

emptied. The provinces grew strong at the expense of the central government, and the *shōen,* the huge estates worked by peasants and owned by families, aristocrats, or religious institutions, grew in power. There was a crisis of public versus private authority.

Large parts of Kyoto were in decline because property owners could no longer

established a new government at Kamakura. In 1192 he was named *shogun,* or chief military commander, by the imperial court. His military power encompassed all of Japan. He was the first shogun of many to coexist with the imperial throne. Japan was ruled by shoguns until well into the nineteenth century.

The Mongols

The Mongols showed great interest in the Japanese archipelago, and in 1266 Kublai Khan sent an emissary to demand submission. The Hojo regent at the time did not acquiesce, but instead mobilized his soldiers. No invasion took place until eight years later, in 1274, when a Mongol fleet appeared off the coast at Kyūshū. Some of the soldiers managed to land, but fortunately for the Japanese, a storm prevented the Mongols from proceeding.

The next invasion took place in 1281 when two fleets totalling 140,000 troops departed simultaneously from China and Korea to conquer Kyūshū. In the meantime, the Hojo regent had impressive defense walls built along the coast. Japanese troops were concentrated on the island of Kyūshū. For the entire summer the defenders were able to repel the Mongol attacks. In the fall a powerful typhoon forced the Mongols to withdraw quickly, using the few ships they had remaining. They immediately began preparations for a third invasion, which was never carried out after Kublai Khan's death in 1294.

The Ashikaga Period (1333–1573)

By the end of the thirteenth century the Japanese economy was in shambles. Contributing factors were the factionalism operative in court and elsewhere, patrimonies, many branches of families dividing estates, the economic strain of the country's defense against the Mongols, and small inheritances, which meant less income for the government. Feudal landowners ruled large portions of land throughout the countryside, and loyalties to the throne were minimal. In 1331 the emperor made an attempt to rid himself of the shoguns but did not succeed. He was exiled instead. In exile he managed to raise an army with the help of his friend Takauji, a member of the Ashikaga family and adversary of the restored Kemmu. He managed to regain power in 1333. From that moment on the emperor would continue to reign with the name of Go-Daigo.

Go-Daigo tried to reintroduce royal rule in 1334 and 1335, when he gave his son, Prince Morinaga, the title of shogun. Takauji was not pleased when he realized that the spoils

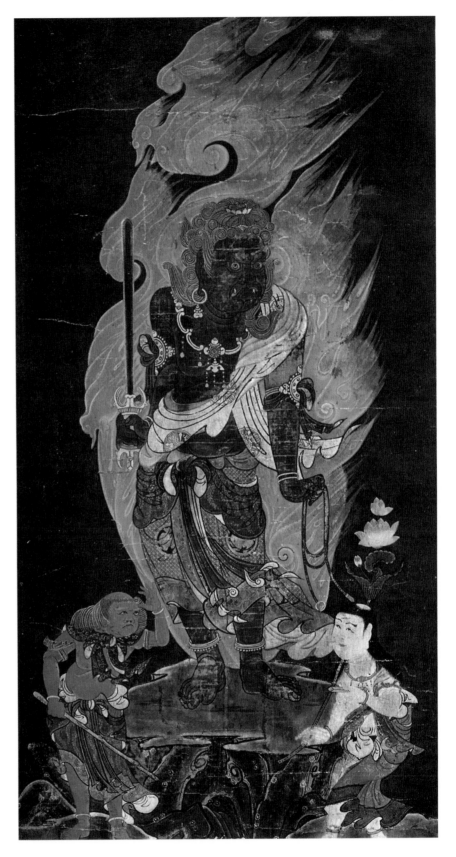

of war had escaped him. He drove off the emperor, setting up Emperor Kūnyū in order to legitimize himself. He restored the shogunate with his Ashikaga family and installed himself as shogun in 1338. Go-Daigo fled to Yoshino in the mountains, where he formed a countergovernment. Japan was reunited in 1392.

Painting on silk of Fudo-Myoo, one of the heavenly kings; made in the twelfth century

1529

Statue of Yoshiyo Minamoto
(1039-1106), the
Japanese Samurai warrior
who shaped the Minamoto clan
into a fighting force

The Ashikaga position was financially supported by this new class, so the family did not become impoverished.

In 1467 a dispute between rival families over the succession to the shogunate led to the Onin War, which was waged for ten years. The Ashikaga Shoguns lost all of their real power, although the last Ashikaga scion was not deposed until 1573. The Fujiwara and even the royal family were left with no political authority. The war continued to rage in the countryside for many more years after order had been restored in Kyoto. Centralized control was nonexistent as Japan faced the civil wars that would cause the period from 1467 until 1568 to be called the Period of the Warring States.

As a result of this constant state of war, unrest grew and the population rose up against their feudal lords. In Yamashiro, for instance, the peasants elected a board of thirty-six men to protect their families. For seven years they managed to keep the tax collectors out. Another group accompanied by Buddhist priests, they kept soldiers, who tried to steal their harvest, at bay with primitive weapons.

Finally, social unrest in Japan brought about the increased importance of the *daimyo,* usually men of locally powerful military families who worked to become peasant leaders. The daimyo would reunite Japan in the sixteenth century, so that when the first Portuguese washed ashore on an island off Kyūshū, around 1543, they encountered a national network of increasingly consolidated domains, organized in military alliances under sophisticated chains of command and civil authority and legitimized by its continued support of the court.

Key Periods in Japanese Art

10,500–400 BC	Jōmon
400 BC–AD 250	Yayoi
250–600	Kofun (Tumulus)
600–710	Asuka (Soga)
710–794	Nara
794–1185	Heian
1185–1333	Kamakura
1333–1573	Ashikaga or Muromachi
1573–1615	Momoyama
1615–1868	Edo

The Ashikaga relocated the residence back to Kyoto, which had been the nominal capital for centuries. Their military authority proved difficult to sustain. There were uneasy alliances throughout this time, which was also a period of new ties to Ming China, dramatic growth in agricultural production, and great cultural achievement.

One cause of the significant economic changes in Japan was the acquisition of great wealth and power by a group of merchants.

A Mongolian leader is served a meal

The Mongols

Nomadic Tribespeople

Bound only to the tribes of their families, the nomadic horsemen and sheepherders called the Mongols had no set domain. They roamed the arid plains of eastern Asia, between the Yablonovy range and the fertile valleys of Shilka River and Lake Baykal to the north and the vast grasslands and Great Wall of China to the south. Most of their domain was 3,000 feet (915 meters) high. Mountains framed them east and west. In the center lay the 500,000-square-mile (1,300,000-square-kilometer) plateau of the Gobi Desert. The coldest desert on earth, its water holes, scant scrub growth, and grass were enough to support occasional herds.

The Mongols left that region over the thir-

Mongols preparing food

Mongolians tending their horses, Chinese painting on silk

teenth and fourteenth centuries to ravage all Asia, Asia Minor, and parts of Europe. They forged a single empire from the Mediterranean to the Pacific.

Chingiz Khan

The Mongol boy Temujin, who was to become the Mongol conqueror Chingiz (Genghis) Khan, was born about 1162 near Lake Baykal. He was thirteen when he suc-

ceeded his father as tribal chief. Yesukai had been the leader of a loosely organized league of Mongol tribes that comprised about thirty thousand families. They tended sheep, hunted, and practiced tribal warfare. They respected personal ability and demanded personal loyalty. Tribal authority was hierarchical. The skilled young chief used these factors and his father's mantle to advantage in his own tribe. As other tribes revolted against his authority, he put them down. By 1190 his leadership was acknowledged throughout Turkestan.

By 1206 Temujin dominated most of Mongolia. He convened a *kurultai*, a gathering of tribal leaders, which he addressed in these historic words: "Those who share my fortune and whose loyalty is as clear as glass, may call themselves Mongols, and their power shall be above everything that lives."

He declared the assembly of families, clans, and tribes to be a single nation. He offered them dominion over the whole world. The gathering proclaimed him Chingiz Khan. (The name came from the

Opposite page: Chingiz Khan surrounded by leaders and servants; he was born around 1162 at Ningsia, China; miniature from the fourteenth century

Chinese *chêng-sze* [valued warrior] and the Turkish *khan* [lord].)

Principles of Conquest

Chingiz Khan ruled from Karakorum. His political principles were simple. There was

ز خورشید شاه گرفتند وحمله پیاده پیاده بارگاه آمدند

چون حرمت رفت ملک جهان هیچ نیرزد مرد خوش باید یا

Women mourning the death of their master. Chingiz Khan said that butchering his enemies and hearing inconsolable women lamenting gave him the greatest pleasure; Persian miniature from the thirteenth century

1534

the blood and eat the entrails of animals, a practice forbidden by custom to many Mongols. Slaughtering was to be done by cutting open the breast of an animal and taking out the heart by hand.

More important was the division of labor for husband and wife. The husband was to hunt and fight; the woman was to handle business affairs and look after the family property.

Every Mongol was accorded equal rights. No Mongol was permitted to enslave another or fight each other. Horse stealing and adultery, regarded as the most serious crimes, were made punishable by death. Less serious infractions were punished with flogging.

Mongol obligations did not include taxes. The army was expected to provide enough booty for arrows and new campaigns.

The Army

Chingiz Khan was a brilliant military strategist and commander. His army was renowned for the discipline of its officers and the skill of its archers. It was divided into units of ten men, obligated to stay together under all circumstances. Ten units of ten men had a leader, as did ten larger units of a hundred. The largest unit was called the horde, which comprised ten thousand soldiers. They were commanded by deputies of the khan, called *orkons*.

Superb horsemen, the Mongol soldiers were all mounted, each bringing two or three horses with him for a campaign. The khan's greatest concern was to have enough mounts at his disposal. Years would often pass before a planned campaign could begin.

The horde's soldiers lived off the land and ate what they found. On long marches through the barren steppes they kept alive with horse blood. Three things about the Mongols amazed their enemies: endurance, mobility, and cruelty to the vanquished.

Chingiz Khan once asked one of his captains what he considered the greatest pleasure for a man.

"Hunting with his people in the steppes, on a beautiful day, with his horse at the gallop," was the answer.

"Nay," said the khan, "the greatest pleasure for a warrior is to trample his foe under foot, to seize his horses and riches, and to hear the wailing of inconsolable women."

The Assault on China

The Chinese had built their Great Wall over thousands of miles to protect them from enemy attack, but the emperors regarded the Mongols as their allies. They assumed Chingiz Khan would go on paying tribute to Peking, as his father had always done.

to be only one ruler. Competitors were to be punished by death. Successors to the khan were to be elected by leaders from the *kurultai*. No individual leader could make peace with an opponent who had not first acknowledged khan authority. The khan himself acknowledged only the authority of the Great Yasa, the code that he created.

He laid down rules that applied to all his subjects. First, he permitted them to drink

When a new emperor, Wai Wang, was crowned, his ministers sent a delegation to Chingiz Khan to demand an oath of fealty. The Mongolian treated the demand with scorn. "Let your emperor know that we don't care whether he regards us as a friend or an enemy," he said. "If he wants to be our friend, then we will let him rule his territories under our authority. But if he would rather have war, then we will fight until one of us is totally destroyed."

After the departure of the delegation, the Mongols began to make arrows and to assemble their horses. In 1200 about three hundred thousand riders crossed the Great Wall. By 1208 they were well established inside China, although the war dragged on for years. The Mongols had particular difficulty in taking the old Chinese cities, surrounded by towers and walls. Every winter the hordes went back to the Mongolian steppes. When summer came, they returned to China to continue plundering. Some generals and high officials impressed by the Mongolian display of power defected to Chingiz Khan. This provided the illiterate Mongols the services of people who could read and write, who could build engines of war, and who were masters of many technologies unknown to them.

In 1213 the khan led his armies to the Shantung Peninsula. Within the year he conquered the Manchus, themselves of Mongolian descent. He took Yenking (Beijing) in 1215, razing most of the city, and installing one of the orkons as administrator. He went on to the Korean Peninsula in 1218, initiating a war that was waged intermittently for thirty years.

The First Western Campaigns
The khan turned his attention to the west in

Ogodai is invested with the highest power; miniature from the fourteenth century

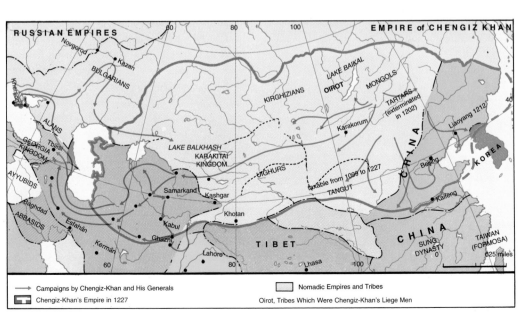

1535

1219. Having been informed that the Muslims in the Islamic kingdoms would be more powerful opponents than the Chinese, he assembled the hordes and declared: "It is necessary for a leader of ten men to be as alert and obedient as the leader of ten thousand men. Anyone who fails in this shall die, together with his wife and children."

His armies invaded the Turkish Empire of Khoresm, a flourishing center of Muslim civilization that included modern Iraq, Iran, and some of Turkestan. They sacked the cities of Bokhara, Samarkand, Tashkent, and Balkh, and went on to take Peshawar (India) and Lahore (Pakistan).

Other hordes moved straight to the heart of Russia in 1222, pillaging their way to the Dnepr River. From the Persian Gulf, they plundered north toward the Arctic Ocean.

Chingiz Khan returned to China to put down a rebellion. He died there on August 18, 1227. In accordance with his wish, his body was taken home to be buried in the shadow of a certain tree.

His empire covered most of Asia, from the Dnepr at the edge of Europe to the China Sea. It was divided among the sons of his primary wife. When it began to crumble, four of his grandsons picked up the pieces.

Ogodai Khan

Each of the khan's three sons was given a khanate, or state. The *kurultai* elected Ogodai, the second son of Chingiz Khan, as his successor. The new great khan remained in the capital of Karakorum to run his own khanate of East Asia, but he sent his hordes in every direction.

The Golden Horde

The horde, predominantly Tatar and commanded by Batu, left Karakorum in 1235. It crossed the Ural River in 1237 to pillage the cities of the Vladimir-Suzdal area in central Russia. By 1240 it sacked Moscow and Kyyiv (Kiev), slaughtering the inhabitants, and went on to Poland and Silesia, razing Lublin and Kraków. In 1241 it burned Breslau (today's Wroclaw). Defeating Bela IV, Arpad king of Hungary, the horde took the city of Pest on the Danube and moved on to take Ragusa on the Adriatic coast. A few weeks later, at Liegnitz (Legnica), on the field of Wahlstatt, Batu defeated an army of Silesians, Poles, and Teutonic Knights. The Mongols suffered heavy losses at the unsuccessful siege of Neustadt. Batu pulled back to southern Russia to recoup.

When the news came later in 1241 that the Great Khan Ogodai was dead, he returned to Karakorum and was chosen as successor. The khanate of Kipchak that Batu had

1536

Travels of Marco Polo

Here are a few passages from the story Marco Polo told his French prison mate in a Genoese jail. Written down originally in French, they were translated into Latin and Italian, and then to many languages. They reflect the nature of Marco Polo's speech. (Note: Prester John, identified as Eyewitness, was a mythical figure of the Middle Ages, said to rule a Christian kingdom somewhere in the East.)

"The Mongols—also called the Tartars—dwelt in Chorcha, but without settled habitations, without towns or fortified places. The Tartars were tributary to Prester John. In time the tribe multiplied so exceedingly that Prester John conceived the plan of dispatching them. The Mongols went to the other side of the mountains, rebelled against Prester John and refused to pay him the customary tribute."

Polo writes that the Mongol leader Chingiz (Genghis) Khan asked for the daughter of Prester John in marriage. The Khan's emissaries received the following reply to that proposal: "How does Chingiz Khan presume to ask for my daughter's hand

Kublai Khan (on the throne) grants Marco Polo a permit to travel through China.

Sixteenth-century Chinese statue, said to represent Marco Polo

when he knows he is only a servant of mine! Leave instantly and never return."

Enraged at this reply, according to Polo, Chingiz (Genghis) Khan collected a large army to fight Prester John, marking the rise of the Mongol world empire.

Khan-balik

Marco Polo lived at the court of the Great Kublai Khan, the grandson of Chingiz (Genghis) Khan, who reigned during his lifetime. He describes Kublai Khan's palace at the khan's new capital in Khan-balik, China.

"In this city is the site of the Khan's vast palace, the form and dimensions of which are as follows. It is larger than any I have ever seen. The roof—adorned with bronze and copper—is very lofty. The sides of the great halls and apartments are ornamented with gold and silver. There are beautiful representations of warriors, women, birds and beasts. The grand hall is extremely long and permits dinners to be served to six thousand people. The palace contains a large number of chambers. The exterior of the roof is adorned with a variety of colors. It is painted so well that it shines like gold. The spaces between the palace walls are ornamented with many handsome trees and meadows in which are kept various kinds of beasts, such as stags, roebuck, and ermine. In the middle, there is a large lake containing all kinds of fish. And the large stream that discharges from the pond is arranged in such a way as to prevent the escape of the fish."

Tibet

"At the end of five days' journey, you reach the province Mangu Khan laid to waste. There are numberless towns and castles, all in a state of ruin. It is possible to travel through this desolate region without encountering lodgings. For that reason travelers must carry their provisions along with them. At the end of that period you come upon a few castles and strong points. It is custom to marry women here [but] the people of these parts are disinclined to marry young women so long as they are virgins, but require, on the contrary that they should have had previous relations with many of the other sex. Upon the arrival of a caravan of merchants, those mothers conduct their daughters to the place and entreat the strangers to enjoy their society. It is a good thing if a merchant sleeps with such a girl, for she can then show whether others have already been her lovers. It is a good thing when many men have slept with her, for she will be married the sooner. It is custom that every woman, before she can marry, has more than twenty spots [ornaments] about her neck. And she who shows the greatest number of them is considered to have attracted the greatest number of men, and is therefore in higher esteem.

A fortress besieged by
Mongols

established over the Russians, still known as
the Golden Horde, suffered a notable defeat
in 1380 at the hands of Dmitry Donskoy,
grand duke of Moscow. The Mongol Tamerlane (unrelated to the clan of Chingiz Khan)
came to the horde's defense, but by 1395 it
had turned against it. The Golden Horde
became the separate khanates of Crimea,
Sibir, Kazan, and Astrakhan, ending in 1480
with the refusal of Ivan III Vasilyevich,
grand duke of Moscow, to pay tribute.

Jagati

Tamerlane had a hand in the khanate of
Turkestan as well. Part of the division of the
Mongol Empire in 1227, it had been given to
Jagati, second son of Chingiz Khan. Lying
just above Tibet, it was an area of prolonged

conflict between nomadic Mongols and the
more settled Muslims of its western region.
In the fourteenth century, khanate authority
went largely unrecognized in that western
section. Tamerlane annexed it in 1370, leaving the khans free to rule the eastern area.

While the Golden Horde stayed in southern Russia, other hordes, under various com-
mands, continued to pillage. Under Hulaku,
grandson of Chingiz Khan, a horde went to
Mesopotamia.

Il-Khan

After Kuyuk's death, the *kurultai* appointed
Mangu, one of Chingiz Khan's grandsons, as
the new khan. His brother Hulaku, self-
proclaimed Il-Khan, was given command of
a horde and the khanate of Persia. By 1231

Mongols cooking their prisoners in pots; the Mongols were notorious for their cruelties

he had led his horde through Iran, Mesopotamia, Armenia, and Georgia.

Il-Khan stormed the Abbasid capital of Baghdad in 1258 and razed it to the ground, massacring more than eight hundred thousand prisoners, men, women and children. Devastation left Baghdad uninhabited for some time. The caliph, sentenced to death, was locked up in his treasure house to await his end.

Il-Khan proceeded to Aleppo and Damascus. When he was on the point of conquering Jerusalem, he received the news of Mangu's death and returned briefly to Karakorum. His brother Kublai had been campaigning in China and had managed to acquire greater prestige than Hulaku. The *kurultai* chose him to replace Mangu as khan.

Il-Khan then returned to his own khanate in Persia (Iran), only nominally recognizing the authority of his brother. (The khanate included parts of today's Iraq, Afghanistan, and Turkmenistan.) Ghazan Khan, who succeeded him in 1295, refused to acknowledge the great khan. He and subsequent khans converted to Islam. Iranian culture prevailed, although Mongolian, Turkish, Persian, and Arabic languages were spoken. With the death of the heirless khan Abu Said in 1395, Iranians broke the region into several states.

Retinue at the Mongol court. The veils of the women are an early sign of Muhammadan influence.

1539

Hulaku and his retinue

Kublai Khan

It was Kublai Khan, grandson of Chingiz Khan, who would take the Mongol Empire to its peak, controlling a fourth of the world.

Appointed Great Khan in 1259, Kublai Khan had spent the previous seven years with Mangu, completing their grandfather's conquest of southern China. Since 1252, they had forced their way to Tibet and Tonkin. Between 1260 and 1279 they had driven the Kin Tatars out of northern China.

Khan-balik

Kublai Khan relinquished his claim to the Mongol Empire outside China, including Karakorum, and subdued rebellious Mongols inside it. He established his capital, Khan-balik (Cambaluc), near Beijing in 1264. The court at Khan-balik was internationally famous. It included the Venetian Marco Polo, whose memoirs would provide an excellent history of the era. Kublai Khan valued him so highly that he made him ambassador and minister.

The new khan considered it more important to have a well-administered empire than a realm of ruined cities. His court was thronged with talented Chinese and Muslims who taught him the art of government they had learned from ancient cultures. He adopted the bureaucratic system of the Chinese but excluded Chinese from positions of authority, replacing them with Mongols.

As Mongol control of the Central Asian trade routes made them increasingly secure, people of all kinds used them more, including missionaries and traders. Although travel enhanced intercultural contact and understanding, it also brought the potential for dispute and civil disruption.

A town besieged by Mongols

The Yüan Dynasty

In 1279 Kublai Khan established the Mongol Yüan dynasty, becoming its first emperor. (It succeeded the Southern Sung dynasty.) He and his successors ruled as Chinese under the dynastic title Yüan, which was accepted by the Chinese.

The emperor encouraged literature and the arts. Although he was a committed Buddhist and made Buddhism the state religion, he permitted the practice of other religions.

Regardless, Mongol rule fomented discord among the Chinese. Chinese officials, primarily Confucians, objected to their reduced status. Peasants objected to new taxes. The crop failures, resultant famine, and inflation, com-

Outer wall of the Medrese in Samarkand. This college was built by Kiwam al-Din around 1420 on the instructions of Ulugh-Beg (cousin of Tamerlane). Astronomy and mathematics were the main subjects taught here.

The Ottoman Sultan Bajazet (The lightning bolt) is taken to Tamerlane; miniature from the fifteenth century

Imperial Expansion

Kublai Khan entered Southeast Asia, forcing allegiance and tribute arrangements on the kings of Burma, Cambodia, and Annan. His expeditions to Java and Japan, however, achieved nothing.

The Mongol Empire reached its greatest size under Kublai Khan.

Tamerlane

After the Great Khan's death, the breakup of the empire accelerated. Several splinter empires had been formed when Tamerlane began his move for power in the 1360s, gaining control of Transoxania by 1370. The Timurid dynasty he established would reign in Transoxania (and later, Iran) through the early sixteenth century.

Born in 1336 at Kesh in Transoxania (Uzbekistan), he was called *Timur Lang* (Timur the Lame) because of a crippled left side. His goal was the reunion of the Mongol Empire as it had been under Chingiz Khan. Not related to the first great khan, he claimed him anyway as forefather and was equally notorious for his own atrocities.

By 1394 he had conquered western Iran, Mesopotamia, Armenia, and Georgia. He sided with and then battled with the Golden Horde over a period of years (1389–1395). He invaded India in 1398, seizing Delhi and massacring its inhabitants after the manner of Chingiz Khan. Moving west, he captured Syria in 1401.

The purpose of his last campaign was to subdue the Mongols on the Volga. He chose a route through Asia Minor that brought him into conflict with the Ottoman Turks. After Tamerlane conquered Ankara, the capital of their powerful empire, and captured Sultan Bajazet (the Lightning Bolt), he brought the sultan along on his expeditions in an iron cage. Bajazet eventually committed suicide, battering his head against the iron bars until he died.

Tamerlane died on February 18, 1405, near Shymkent (modern Kazakhstan), while leading an expedition to conquer China. He had extended Mongolian power from India to the Mediterranean Sea.

His descendant, Babur, founded the Mughal dynasty of India in 1526.

Modern family of nomads; their lifestyle has not changed a lot since the days of Chingiz Khan.

bined with Huang He floods, led to widespread civil discontent and provincial rebellion in the 1330s and 1340s. By the 1360s, a former Buddhist monk named Chu Yuanchang gained control of the Yangtze Valley.

The Mongol Yüan dynasty survived in China until 1368, when the Chinese replaced it with the Ming dynasty. In 1371, Chu Yuanchang captured Beijing. Remaining Mongols were forced to return to Mongolia.

The Kingdoms of Africa

Regional Powers

Northeast Africa
The Empire of Nubia (Cush)
(1000 BC–AD 350)

The kingdom Nubia ruled the middle Nile from the eighth to the fourth centuries after 1,800 years of Egyptian domination. Information is limited since Nubian writing has yet to be deciphered, but in 725 BC the Nubian king Piankhy conquered Egypt, creating its twenty-fifth dynasty. Nubian rule from the Mediterranean to Ethiopia lasted about a hundred years. The empire lost control to Assyria's Assurbanipal in the 660s BC, but Nubian influence is evident in the black pharaohs depicted in Egyptian tombs. The Nubians retreated south to their capital, Meroë, continuing their independent and advanced civilization until conquered by the Ethiopians.

Bronze head
from the Benin
Empire

The Cush traded iron, gold, ivory, and elephants not just in Africa, but to Greece and Rome, exchanging ambassadors with the Roman emperor Nero. They destroyed Roman outposts at Elephantine, Philae, and Aswân in 25 and 24 BC, precipitating a border agreement between Cush and Roman Egypt. (Strabo, the Roman historian, notes a "Queen Candace" leading the attack on Philae. *Candace* was the Cushite word for queen; it was not an individual name but

1543

Caravan trade through the Sahara Desert was the main source of income for the peoples in Africa. Trade contacts resulted in the spreading of Islam over the African continent.

The city of Timbuktu in Mali used to be a metropolis for trans-Sahara trade. Caravans from the north came here to buy the products (including slaves) of the African countries.

probably indicated a female ruler was in command.)

The people of Nubia were converted to Christianity in the sixth century AD and established three new kingdoms, Nobatia, Mukurra, and Alodia. The region, largely independent for some 2,000 years, was conquered by the Arabs in the fourteenth centu-

ry AD. Alodia would resist Islam until the sixteenth century. In 1820 Egypt would reassert control.

The Kingdom of Aksum (AD 50–1100)

The ancient kingdom of Aksum was founded about AD 50 by the Amhara of the northern Ethiopian highlands, a people partly Semitic in origin. The new rulers established the Solomonid dynasty, claiming direct descent from the biblical king Solomon and the queen of Sheba.

The empire, centered at Aksum, traded via the Red Sea with Greece, Rome, and India. In the third and sixth centuries AD Aksum also dominated Yemen on the Arabian Peninsula.

In the early fourth century the king Ezana was converted to Christianity by two Syrian Christians, Frumentius and Aedesius. He made Christianity one of the state religions in Aksum. Surrounded first by pagans and then by Muslims, Aksum fought wars for both religious and commercial reasons. As Aksum declined over the seventh century, its kings forged alliances with the Christian emperors in Byzantium. By the early tenth century, the Solomonid dynasty was replaced by the Zagwe, ruling family of the central plateau region of Lasta.

West Africa
The Empire of Ghana (AD 400–1240)

Earliest known empire in the sub-Sahara,

1544

Ghana was founded about AD 400. Its Iron Age culture, learned from the West African Nok people, dated back to about 250 BC. The kingdom lay between the upper Senegal and Niger Rivers, northwest of modern Ghana. Extending from Timbuktu on the Niger to the Atlantic Ocean, it was well positioned for trade.

Ghanian gold, mined in the Wangara region in the Senegal basin, was shipped north in exchange for Saharan salt. Ghana also exported kola nuts, ivory, and slaves. It grew wealthy on trade between the eighth and eleventh centuries. At stations along the trade routes it taxed salt, textiles, copperware, Egyptian horses, and tools from Italy and Germany. It established an extensive system to collect income tax as well.

Contemporary chroniclers of Ghana, Ibn Khaldun and El Idrissi, describe life there as one of great luxury. The populace wore woolen, silk, and velvet clothing. The royal palaces were decorated with sculpture, painting, and glasswork. The hundreds of horses of the royal stables walked on carpets and were tied with silk ropes.

Ghana reached its peak under the Soninke elite about 1050. Considerable information comes from the 1068 *Book on the Roads and Kingdoms*. It was compiled by Córdoba (Spain) geographer El Bekri from the first-hand reports of travelers and merchants. He wrote: "Ghana consists of two cities situated on a plain. One . . . inhabited by Muslims is very large and has twelve mosques. The city where the king resides lies at a distance of six miles (10 kilometers) and is called al-Ghaba, which means 'the forest.' The region between the two cities is covered with houses that are built of stone and wood. The king has interpreters, a treasurer, and chooses most of his viziers [high executive officers] from among the Muslim population. The Negro's religion is pagan and consists of idol worship. All gold nuggets found in the mines belong to the king, but he gives the gold dust to his subjects. The king of Ghana can raise an army of 200,000 men, 40,000 of whom are armed with bow and arrow."

Archaeological digs since 1914 in Kumbi Saleh (southernmost city in modern Mauritania) have uncovered the ruins of stone dwellings and warehouses. Inscriptions on walls, mosques, and tombs indicate this to be the city that El Bekri described. Kumbi Saleh was the commercial center of the empire.

The capital city, Ghana, was conquered and plundered in 1076 by the Almoravids, a militant Muslim sect of the Sanhaja Berbers in Morocco.

The kingdom continued to disintegrate as West African peoples withdrew allegiance and formed independent kingdoms. Around 1200, people from Takrur took control of Ghana. Takrur was challenged by the Mandinka from another small kingdom, Kangaba, on the upper Niger. In 1240 Mandinka king Sundiata Keita defeated the Takrur at the battle of Kirina and razed the city of Ghana.

Wooden door of the palace of the kings of Songhai, found in the north of the present-day state of Dahomey

Wooden head,
an example
of Bambara art

Wooden statue
from the Cameroon
region

1546

The Kingdom of Mali (AD 1250–1400)

Sundiata Keita, founder of the kingdom of Mali, had assumed the throne of a small state on the upper Niger River in 1230. He conquered neighboring tribal domains (notably the Susu in 1235). To the Mande people of Sierra Leone, he was *Mari Jata* (the Great), as he is still known today. He introduced cotton cultivation and textile manufacture to the empire, but its main economic resource lay in trade. His Dyula traders established outposts throughout western Africa, creating links to the long-distance trade routes between Asia and Africa and, via the Mediterranean, to Europe. Sundiata developed an efficient system to tax trade. A succession of capable Muslim Mali kings followed his death in 1260.

Conquering the Niger River cities of Timbuktu and Gao, Mansu "emperor"

Congo Musa (1307–1332) made Mali into a vast empire between 1312 and 1337. Traveling via Cairo with a caravan of thousands of people (some historians estimate 60,000), he distributed so many gifts of gold that he caused inflation throughout Egypt. In Mecca he met the Arabian poet and architect Es Saheli, whom he took back to Mali. Es Saheli encouraged the empire to import Muslim teachers to build schools and a university in Timbuktu.

An eyewitness account of the Mali Empire in the mid-fourteenth century is attributed to Ibn Battuta of Tangiers. An adventurous Arab traveler, he had visited India, China, Indonesia, and Turkestan before arriving in the Mali capital, Niani, in 1353. Mansa Süleyman had succeeded his brother Congo Musa as emperor. Ibn Battuta comments: "The sultan's daily dress is a red velvet tunic. He is preceded by musicians, who carry gold

The large mosque of Djenné in Mali. The building is completely made of clay.

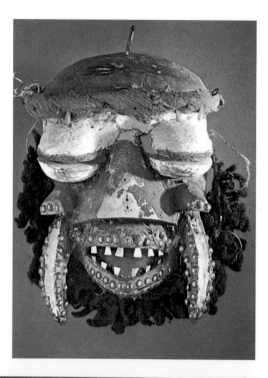

Painted wooden mask decorated with nails, which was used in funeral dances; from Mali

Wooden head, from the Benin Empire

give it to a white man they trust to guard until the legal heirs come to claim it."

In 1400 Niani was conquered by the Songhai. A smaller Mali kingdom continued to exist in the Mande domain. It was there when the Portuguese entered in 1494.

The Kingdom of the Songhai (1400–1600)

After seizing Niani, Sunni Ali (1465–1492) incorporated eastern Mali and the middle Niger region. He formed individually governed regional provinces, an army, and a Niger River navy, using the military to capture the powerful city of Djenné in 1473. Askia the Great Muhammad Mama du Touré (1464–1528) succeeded him in 1493.

Three years later Askia went on a pilgrimage to Mecca. (Most Songhai had become Muslim about AD 1000.) He was made caliph (Islamic leader) of western Sudan. He extended the empire by conquest from his capital and trade center Gao, east to Lake Chad and west almost to the Atlantic. He conquered the important commercial city of Agadez on the edge of the Sahara, seizing the salt mines under its control. He had irrigation canals dug in the region, making desert land arable. The trade routes to Tripoli and the Nile Valley converged at Agadez. Slaves were part of the trade, sold to the Arabs in the north. In 1513 he gained even more control over trade, annexing Kano, a rising city on the Hadejia River, tributary of Lake Chad.

Askia made Timbuktu an even greater cultural center than it had been under the Mali. The Songhai Empire was described by sixteenth-century scholar Leo Africanus in his *History and Description of Africa*: "The inhabitants of Timbuktu are very rich, in particular the foreigners who have settled here. There are many judges, physicians, and scribes, all of whom receive good salaries from the king."

Indigenous authors gained prominence. 'Abd al-Rahmān al-Sadi wrote *Tarikh as-Sudan (Chronicle of the Sudan)*. Ahmad Baba wrote works on Islamic law that are still in use today. In 1851, German traveler Heinrich Barth discovered handwritten translations of Plato and Aristotle and treatises on astronomy and mathematics in the Baguirmi area, south of Lake Chad.

The Songhai Empire was brought down by a Moroccan cavalry invasion in 1591. (The Moroccans, learning that the gold mines they sought were farther south, left the Sudan plains for the lower forests. Native guerrilla skill eventually drove them out.)

Minor kingdoms—the Macina, Gonja, Ségou, Kaarta—arose, vying to fill the

and silver guitars, and followed by three hundred armed slaves. When he sits down, they play trumpets, drums and horns. The blacks are rarely unjust and they detest injustice more than any other people. Their sultan has no mercy for anyone who is guilty of the least bit of injustice. Complete freedom reigns in the land. Neither travelers nor the inhabitants have reason to fear robbers or violent men. They do not seize the possessions of a white man who dies in their land, not even if he possesses great wealth. On the contrary, they

power vacuum left by Songhai. None achieved dominance.

Kanem-Bornu (800–1846)

The Saifawa converted to Islam in the eleventh century. Expanding by conquest, they bordered on the Niger River to the west, Wadai to the east, and the Fezzan to the north by the thirteenth century. The Bulala people drove the dynasty west into the Bornu region in the next century, retaining control of Kanem themselves. Under Ali Ghaji, the Saifawa dynasty continued its empire from a new capital, Ngazargamu. Mai Idris Alooma, who reigned from about 1580 to 1617, greatly increased imperial power using firearms purchased from the Ottoman Turks. He established a control over the trade routes to Egypt that would be weakened by the eighteenth century. The empire was taken over by Wadai in 1846.

Hausa City-states (900–1591; peak: 1400)

The Hausa, a racially diverse people, estab-

Wooden statue
from the coastal region
of Cameroon

Wooden mask
of the
Senufo, Ivory Coast

1549

Ritual mask of the Kuba tribe in Zaire, decorated with embroidery and shells

Wooden bust of the Senufo; from the ancient kingdom of old Mali, present-day Ivory Coast

lished several independent city-states in the late ninth century. All of them lay between the domains of Songhai on the Niger River and Kanem-Bornu, around Lake Chad. The states were Biram, Daura, Zaria, Rano, Gobir, Katsina, and Kano. The last two were major urban centers of commerce, part of the trans-Saharan trade. In the fourteenth century they all became Muslim and were repeatedly subjected to conquest by the larger kingdoms of West Africa.

Kingdom of Benin
(c.1100–1897; peak: 1450)
The Edo or Bini people founded the king-dom of Benin in the twelfth century. Its *obas* (kings) ruled from Benin City over most of what is today southern Nigeria. Oba Ozolua (c.1480–1504) established trade (including slaves) with Portugal that continued through the eighteenth century. Benin was annexed to British Nigeria in 1897.

Kingdom of Ashanti (peak: 1750)
Ashanti tribes formed a confederation in the early eighteenth century. As they tried to subdue the Fanti tribes in 1807, they encountered the British and battled both until 1826. Their capital, Kumasi, was burned in the Ashanti-British War of 1873–1874. Prempeh

I, chosen head chief in 1888, was captured in 1896 and sent by the British to the Seychelles Islands in the Indian Ocean. He was reinstated in 1926 in recognition of Ashanti loyalty.

The Kingdom of Oyo (peak: 1750)

The Yoruba people established the kingdom of Oyo, between the Volta and Niger Rivers, which flourished in the middle of the seventeenth century. By the early nineteenth century it collapsed into numerous petty kingdoms before falling under British control.

Kingdom of Dahomey (peak: 1800)

The kingdom of Dahomey was founded on the coast of the Gulf of Guinea in the early seventeenth century. From its capital, Abomey, it expanded over the next century, notably through King Agaja. He seized the towns of Allada and Ouidah and began supplying slaves to Europe. King Gézo, reigning from 1818 to 1858, added inland territory as the French arrived on the coast. The French defeated the next king, Béhanzin, making Dahomey a French colony. (It is now the country Benin.)

East Africa

The Port-states (1200–1400)

The huge Bantu migration at the turn of the millennium (AD 1000) resulted in an influx of Bantu to the region. They assimilated the indigenous San peoples into their various clans. Arabs, interested in trade, appeared along the coast and on the island of Zanzibar. Through the Red Sea and the Persian Gulf they connected with the Asian continent. This was important in the development of several city-states. Arab traders established ports, colonizing the coast and merging with the resident Bantu population. They developed a new culture and language, Swahili, which became the common tongue. They exported gold, ivory, and slaves, many of them Bantu. The ruling classes were Arab-Africans. The resultant city-states, still a feature of African ethnic diversity and conflict, lined the coast: Mogadishu, Mombasa, Malindi, Lamu, Kilwa, Pate, and Sofala.

The Inland Kingdoms (1200–1400)

Inland, people of unknown origin moved

Statue of the goddess Odudua and her retinue, from the Yoruba tribe

1552

down the Nile to settle the interlake areas. They established complex societies over the fourteenth century. Like the port city-states, the new cultures loom large in today's headlines. As the people of Rwanda and Burundi battle each other for survival, there is new interest in the question of their ancestry. The Tutsi are generally assumed to be descendants of the Cushites.

Bachwezi had created a kingdom between Lakes Victoria and Edward in the late fourteenth century. Luo people from the Sudan took it over around 1500. The Luo established Ankole, Buganda, and Karagwe. The Bachwezi went south (to Rwanda), establishing another cattle-culture kingdom over the indigenous and settled Bantu peoples (called Bututsi) by the sixteenth century.

Central Africa

The Mwene Mutapa Empire (c.800–c.1800)

Probably the earliest and most advanced civilization of Central Africa was begun by the Karanga people. They are the descendants of the Bantu and the ancestors of the Shona living in Zimbabwe today. They found and exploited vast deposits of gold, using it to establish trade and the Mwene Mutapa Empire.

About 1100 the Karanga began constructing the elaborate stone complex called the Great Zimbabwe, completing it 800 years later. A massive 30-foot- (9-meter-) high stone wall still encloses most of its ruins near Masvingo today. An "acropolis" dominates the scene from a nearby hill. It was the religious and political center of an empire the Portuguese called Monomotapa. The realm lay opposite the island of Madagascar on the Indian Ocean coast. Mwene Mutapa controlled the land between the Zambezi and Limpopo Rivers within a hundred years. It reached far inland to the edge of the Kalahari Desert and divided toward the end of the fifteenth century, forming a kingdom called Changamire.

The Portuguese, who had been colonizing the coast farther north in Mozambique since 1500, made Mwene Mutapa a vassal state in 1629. Changamire conquered most of it by the end of that century. Changamire, in turn, was destroyed in 1834 by Ngoni soldiers

Wooden statue of the Yoruba tribe, depicting the reception of a European

under Zwangendaba, on their twenty-year march north to modern Tanzania.

The Kongo Kingdom (peak: 1500)

On the opposite coast of Africa, the Kongo king Wene established a kingdom in the fourteenth century. His successors created a complex system of government based on the election of a ruler from among his descen-

Wooden throne from the royal palace of the Songhai

dants. The realm reached south to the Loge River and inland from the Atlantic to the first long north-south river, the Kwango. It fell to the Portuguese slave traders in the 1600s.

The Luba Empire (peak: 1500)

The Luba chief Kongolo began a conquest in the heart of Central Africa east of Lake Tanganyika about 1500. He dominated an area east to the upper Kasai River, organizing those he subdued into the Luba Empire. It soon divided, plagued by dynastic squabbles.

The Lunda Empire (peak: 1750)

About 1600 one of Kongolo's sons founded

1553

For centuries, gold dust and gold nuggets were used as payment in the Kingdom of Asante. The pieces of gold had to be weighed to determine the exact value, and for that purpose every tradesman owned his own bronze weights. The weight depicted here is shaped as a human. Others could be shaped as animals, or could be depicting abstract symbols.

a separate dynasty and a new state, the Lunda Empire, on Luba's southern border. That divided, in turn, into the Bemba Kingdom, Kasanje, and Kazembe. Largest of the Luba-Lunda states, Kazembe dominated the Katanga plateau between 1750 and 1850.

Southern Africa
The Zulumfecane (1830–1840) and Results

Indigenous San (Bushman) and Khoikhoi (Hottentot) yielded to incoming and more powerful Bantu immigrants to southern Africa by AD 1000. Divided linguistically, the descendants of the eastern branch include the Shona, the Xhosa, the Kikuyu, and the Zulu. (Bantu of the western linguistic branch include today's Herero and Tonga people in Angola, Namibia, and Botswana.)

As the century turned, so did the ways of the military strategist and the Bantu Zulu ruler Shaka. He had previously attempted to unite the neighboring Bantus in what is now the South African province of KwaZulu/-Natal, but later attacked them. The era of warfare he initiated, called *mfecane* (Zulu for "crushing"), put great pressure on the tribes. Over the next decade he ousted peoples from their lands, set off massive social dislocation and migration, and caused the creation of new kingdoms. His tribal victims left the area in all directions, taking with them his successful new battle techniques.

In historical sequence, Ndwandwe chief Sobhuza went north in the 1820s, establishing the Swazi Kingdom. Moshesh formed the Basotho kingdom in what is today Lesotho. The Ngoni followed over the course of twenty years. Under Zwangendaba, they destroyed the Changamire in 1834. Fourteen years later they created five warlike kingdoms. Under Soshangane they founded the Gaza Empire in 1830. The Kololo under Sebetwane also went north, seizing Barotseland (modern Zambia). The Ndebele under Mzilikazi founded Matabeleland (in today's Zimbabwe) in 1837.

The Zulus remaining on their home territory were subject to the onslaughts of whites. Under King Dingane, and later Cetshwayo, they withstood conquest until their defeat by the British in 1879.

The Green Mosque in ancient Nicaea

The Advent of the Ottoman Empire

The Rise of Turkic Power in the Fifteenth and Sixteenth Centuries

Muslim Seljuk Turks, a Turkoman clan of the Oghuz tribe from the Siberian steppes, converted to Islam in the tenth century. Under Togrul Beg, protector of the Sunni caliph of Baghdad, they conquered most of Iran and Iraq. (Despite opposition from the Shia Muslims, they would rule until Mongols under Chingiz [Genghis] Khan

View of Brusa,
with the Green Mosque
and the Mausoleum
rising high above the houses.
The first six sultans
of the Turkish Empire are
buried in this town.

sacked Baghdad in 1258.) In 1071 they defeated the army of Christian Byzantium at the Battle of Manzikert.

Later in the eleventh century the Seljuk Turks invaded Asia Minor. With the assistance of Turkoman nomads, they established the sultanate of Rum. They ruled central Anatolia from the capital they set up at Konya. The nomads, under nominal Rum auspices, created minor states that fought the Byzantines and each other until Rum itself was subjugated by the Mongols in 1243.

Osman (1258–1324)

Ertogrul (who died about 1280) was chief of a Turkish tribal realm in northwestern Anatolia. His people had fled Turkestan for Asia Minor in advance of the Mongol hordes. According to legend, he dreamed that a crescent moon rose from the bosom of his beloved. Interpreting it as a prophecy of their future greatness, his people adopted the crescent moon as their symbol. Ertogrul's son Osman (Othman or Ottoman) fulfilled that promise, founding the Ottoman dynasty. Taking the towns of Eskisehir, Bilecik,

Yarhisar, and Yenisehir from the Byzantines, he made them the base of the Ottoman Empire that would only be dissolved in 1918, at the end of World War I.

Orhan (reigned 1324–1360)

Osman's son Orhan established a small kingdom in the eastern part of the Byzantine Empire. He conquered Nicaea, Nicomedia, and, in 1326, the Byzantine provincial capital, Bursa. He developed Bursa as an Islamic religious center, achieving both administrative and military control over former Christian areas. He allowed his soldiers to be hired as mercenaries by the Byzantines in return for the right to raid the Byzantium-controlled regions of Thrace and Macedonia. John VI Cantacuzene used Ottoman troops to gain the Byzantine throne in 1347 and wedded his daughter to Orhan. Orhan's dynasty bought or married into Turkoman territory as well.

The Making of the Ottoman Empire

One night in 1356, Orhan's son, Süleyman, rafted across the Bosporus in secret.

Accompanied only by sixty soldiers, he reached Tzimpo, the headquarters of the Byzantine minister. By the time the Christians learned of their arrival, Süleyman and his men had already left, stealing the entire Byzantine fleet. The Ottomans were now a small naval power. Süleyman subsequently conquered Tzimpo and several other territories.

Despite Süleyman's conquests, it was his brother, Murad I, who succeeded Orhan. With the conquest of the city of Adrianople in 1361, Murad began almost three decades of campaigns in Europe. Breaking with dynastic precedent, he also attacked his

Murad I
reigned from 1359 to 1389.
Turkish miniature.

Turkish rivals in Anatolia, using Christian soldiers. He was killed in the Battle of Kossovo in 1389, but his son Bayezid I won that battle, defeating an allied Bulgarian, Bosnian, and Serbian army.

Janissaries

Murad I was the founder of the elite military unit called the Janissaries. (Its name is a Latin corruption of the Turkish *yeni cheri* [new army].) To avoid problems of familial loyalty, he bought slaves and made them soldiers. He brought prisoners of war to Bursa for military service. He demanded Christian children as tribute, putting them in training camps and indoctrinating them in the ways of Islam. The Janissaries, eventually num-

Minaret of the Mosque of
Bayezid II in Istanbul, construction
of which was started in 1501

1557

MA HOM TES CELI

Skandebeg was a
national hero of the
Albanians.
He withstood a siege by
Sultan Murad II in 1450.

bering 40,000, played a large part in the success of the empire. They did, however, bring with them a considerable risk, since a Janissary revolt was always enough to bring down a sultan.

Bayezid I, Sultan of Turkey (reigned 1389–1402/3)

Bayezid I (or Yildirim) was the first of the dynasty to use the title of sultan. He established the Ottoman Empire his father had begun in the Balkans and Anatolia. He was nicknamed *Yildirim* (lightning) for the speed of his conquests, spanning only three years in Bulgaria, Serbia, and Macedonia. He subdued most of the Anatolian Turkoman principalities, undermining Muslim support for the empire, as he expanded its territory. Using Christian mercenaries, he besieged Constantinople for a decade. In 1402 the Mongol Timur, or Timurlenk (Tamerlane is his Anglicized name), invaded Anatolia and captured Sultan Bayezid. Timur put him on exhibit in an iron cage, driving Bayezid to suicide by beating his head against the bars.

Civil War

Timur did not subdue the Turkish Empire.

He handed over its administration to Bayezid's four sons. The outcome was nineteen years of internecine civil war. The youngest son, Mehmed (Muhammad, reigned 1413–1421), finally brought the empire under his control by killing off his brothers and fighting Christians and Turks alike in Europe and Anatolia. He died in 1421 and was succeeded by his eighteen-year-old son, Murad II.

Murad II, Sultan of the Ottoman Empire (1421–1444 and 1446–1451)

Murad II reestablished Ottoman authority over regions lost to Timur, going as far as the Danube in Europe. He unsuccessfully besieged Byzantium with his Janissaries. After he took Thessalonica from the Venetians in 1430, his success became a matter of concern to Christians in western Europe. Pope Eugenius IV called for a crusade against him. An army of Crusaders commanded by Wladyslaw III of Poland entered the Balkans, to be defeated by the Turks at the Battle of Varna in 1444.

Mehmed II, Sultan of Ottoman Turkey (reigned 1444–1446 and 1451–1481)

Murad II retired temporarily in 1444. His son Mehmed II (called the conqueror "Fatih") took over until Murad returned to the throne in 1446. Two years later, Murad defeated Hungarian commander János Hunyadi at the Second Battle of Kosovo. After Murad's death in 1451, Mehmed assembled an army of 250,000 Janissaries, built a fleet of 280 ships, and had enormous cannons cast. In 1453 he laid siege to Constantinople.

The beleaguered city was ruled by the young Constantine XI Paleologus. His claim to the throne was contested and he had never been crowned. With little money and few troops, Constantine told his followers: "My trust is in God. If it pleases Him that you make peace, I shall rejoice in your friendship, and if He delivers Byzantium into your hands, I shall submit myself to His decisions. But as long as His will is not fully clear to me, it is my duty to live and die in the defense of my people."

Constantine sought help from the Christian West, but the pope was only willing to call for a crusade if the Orthodox Church would merge with the Roman Church. Genoa alone responded, sending two ships to his assistance.

At dawn on May 29, 1453, Mehmed II, armed with an iron club, led 10,000 Janissaries in the attack. Behind them came a squad of executioners who beheaded anyone who tried to flee. Byzantine resistance collapsed and plundering began at once. Toward midday, Mehmed made a formal entry on horseback through the gate of St. Roman, symbolically proceeding into the Hagia Sophia (Church of the Holy Wisdom).

The New Rome (Greek rival to the Latin seat of Christianity) had fallen to Muslims. Constantinople would henceforth be known as Istanbul, the capital of the Turkish Empire. Mehmed II subsequently converted the Hagia Sophia and many other churches into mosques.

Mehmed II went on to conquer Greece, Serbia, Bosnia, Albania, and most of the region around the Black Sea. In May 1481

In 1448 Murad II won a victory over the Christians led by János Hundayi near Kosovo, but he did not succeed in fully subjecting the Albanians

The Dominicans, Hounds of the Lord

Dominic in front of the stake

Dominic de Guzman was born in Caleruega, Castile, about 1170. The son of a well-to-do family, he studied theology and philosophy at the University of Palencia. In 1195, at the age of twenty-five, he was ordained as a priest. A year later he was made canon of the Cathedral of Osma, in Castile. His first appearance on the international scene was said to have been a journey that he made in 1203 with his superior, Didacus of Acebes, bishop of Osma, perhaps to Denmark, where the bishop was to perform the marriage of the Castilian king to a Scandinavian princess.

En route home, Dominic traveled through the Languedoc region of southern France, where he observed significant religious controversy among the inhabitants. At issue was the Albigensian heresy. This postulated a dualist doctrine of good and evil, contending that each had eternal and equal power and saw creation itself as evil. The Albigenses had separated themselves from the Catholic Church, and Dominic observed that they were well organized and articulate, readily able to convince others of their views. He

Relief on the tomb of Dominic depicting a scene relating to his life

nd Didacus determined to oppose the eresy and began to preach. Shortly afterward, the bishop was obliged to return to his ee. Dominic stayed on to preach the orthoox Catholic doctrine in fiery language with ttle success. His farewell sermon states: For many years, I have exhorted you with ove and taught you with entreaties and rayers. But there is a Spanish proverb that ays: 'Where no blessings come, tempests vill come instead.' I shall put kings and clerymen in arms against you, and they shall ome to punish you."

The punishers were already on the way. A roup of bishops, noblemen, and laymen escended on Languedoc and massacred nen, women, and children.

Dominic concluded that a new religious rder was necessary to preserve the unity of ne Church. He went to Rome to obtain conent for his plan, but the pope did not conider it a good idea, as the ecclesiastical uthorities were very cautious in granting ermission for new orders. He advised the riest to join the order of St. Benedict, St. Augustine, or St. Bernard. Dominic and a ew companions preached instead from a ouse and a church at Prouille, near 'oulouse, and established a convent in 1206. n 1216 Pope Honorius granted ecclesiastical pproval for the Order of Friars Preachers.

The Dominicans preferred to establish hemselves within the walls of cities, where hey found the largest audiences. In some hurches they held masses and festivals in nonor of local saints. They founded lay chools and visited the faithful to discuss roblems of their daily lives. Their activities extended to the highest levels of society and government, but Dominic's main purpose vas to watch over the purity of Catholic docrine. In contrast with his contemporary, St. Francis, he emphasized education, encouragng his monks to study in Paris, Bologna, Rome, Toulouse, and Madrid. He established riories in Rome, France, and Spain. Dominic died in Bologna on August 6, 1221. Canonized (declared a saint) in 1234, his traitional feast day is August 8. Dominican cholars include Albertus Magnus and Thomas Aquinas. The entire Church talked bout the *domini canes* (the hounds of the Lord).

Later on, the Dominicans were to be the Iriving force behind the establishment of the nquisition.

on the verge of invading Italy, he sent a Turkish fleet of 170 galleys to besiege the island of Rhodes in the Aegean Sea. Under Pierre d'Aubusson, the Knights of St. John had turned the island into an impregnable fortress. Two months later, they forced the Turks to withdraw, an important but costly victory for the Christians. Nine thousand people died and fifteen thousand were wounded.

Mehmed II attempted to build on the fruits

Mehmed II reigned from 1451 to 1481 and built the Fatih Mosque in Constantinople, where he is also buried

of his conquests. Well educated, he was an excellent administrator. He rebuilt Constantinople. He promulgated the *Kanun Nameh*, a codification of Ottoman law.

Mehmed saw the sultan as head of the empire, selecting one of his sons to succeed him. He prevented the kind of war that occurred among the sons of Bayezid by decreeing: "When my sons and grandsons come to the throne, they may have their brothers killed, in order to ensure that the world remains at peace." (He also established a system for locking up the younger sons in a windowless wing of the palace.)

Next in rank were the *beys*, who collected

taxes and recruited soldiers in the various provinces. Mehmed II had a tax register compiled in which they recorded the values of sources of income, tax rates, and penalties.

He formed a group of advisers called the *ulama* (Arabic for wise). All these men had

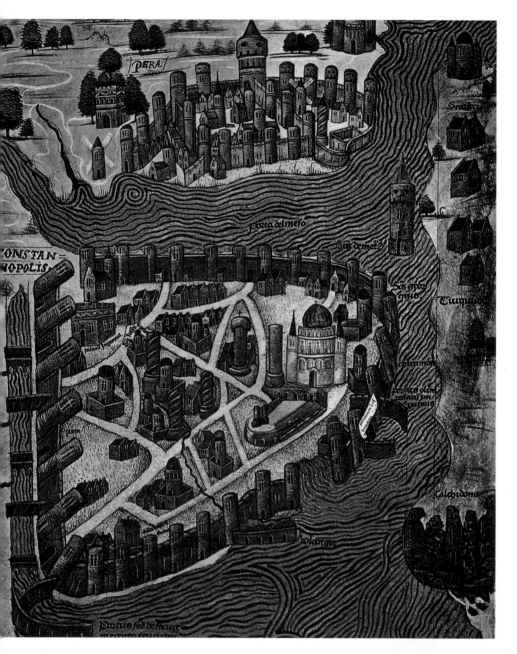

Plan of Constantinople before occupation by the Turks

mastered three languages: Turkish, Arabic, and Persian. They were required to be well versed in the Koran, the scripture of Islam. This was regarded as the infallible recording of God's message to the Prophet Muhammad. Not only religious practices but all matters of law and science were derived from the Koran.

Bayezid II, Sultan of Turkey (reigned 1481–1512)
Bayezid II, son of Mehmed II, succeeded him in 1481. He continued building mosques

and his empire, seizing Hungary, Poland, Venice, Egypt, and Persia, in turn. Eventually halting new conquests to focus on consolidation, he was forced to abdicate by his youngest son, Selim I.

Selim I (reigned 1512–1520)
Sultan Selim I was more attracted by the great Muslim empires in the East than by Europe. First on his list was Persia, with its vast treasury. Its *shah* (ruler) kept retreating from Selim's firepower. Shah Ismait finally joined battle on August 23, 1514. Selim put his cannons to use, annihilating the Persians.

Two years later, Selim began war against the Mamluk Empire in Syria, Palestine, Egypt, and Arabia. *Mamluk* means slave in Arabic. The Mamluk Empire had its origin in a thirteenth-century Janissary-style militia in Egypt. A sultan had formed a bodyguard of Kipchak Turk slaves from the Black and Caspian Sea areas. They rebelled in 1252, killed the sultan, Ayyubid, and established their own government. The Mamluks were Muslims, but insufficiently committed to the faith, in Selim's view.

Selim overcame the Syrian Mamluks without much effort, but those in Egypt resisted until 1517. In keeping with his campaign purpose, the victorious sultan showed no interest in the pyramids and monuments of the pharaohs, visiting the mosques instead. Selim reigned for eight years. His son, Süleyman, was on the Ottoman throne for forty-six years.

Süleyman the Magnificent; Sultan of Turkey (reigned 1520–1566)
Süleyman I succeeded his father in 1520. Over his long reign, Süleyman brought the Ottoman Empire to its peak, crossing the Danube to take Hungary, seizing the rest of Anatolia and parts of Iraq. His realm ran from the Balkans to the Middle East and Persia. In Arabia, it included the coasts of the Red Sea and the Persian Gulf.

The Mediterranean
In 1522 Süleyman drove the Knights of St. John of Jerusalem from the island of Rhodes, forty-one years after they had stood off Mehmed II. His galleys dominated the Mediterranean Sea. He controlled its shores everywhere outside of Europe. His domain eventually reached to northern Africa. In 1551 he captured the city of Tripoli.

European Campaigns
Süleyman first invaded Hungary a year after gaining the throne. He seized the city of

Belgrade. (At the end of World War II, this would be made the capital of Yugoslavia. As of 1996, it was under Serbian control.) In 1526 the sultan reinvaded Hungary, killing King Louis II and defeating the Hungarian army at Mohács. Three years later he took the side of John I Zápolya, who had been elected king of Hungary by its nobles. John's claim was challenged by Austria's Archduke Ferdinand. Süleyman drove Ferdinand back into Vienna and then unsuccessfully besieged the city in 1529.

In 1541 Süleyman invaded Hungary again, capturing Buda (across the Danube from the city of Pest) and incorporating the country into his empire. He would die while besieging the Hungarian city of Szigetvár on September 7, 1566.

European royalty sought Süleyman's assistance. In 1535 he allied with French king Francis I against Holy Roman Emperor Charles V, opening the Mediterranean littoral to French trade. When Francis was subsequently imprisoned in Madrid, he appealed to Süleyman for support. The sultan sent back an arrogant reply. Francis, once back in Paris, bore no grudge. Friendly diplomatic relations with the Turks would be maintained for centuries.

Mehmed II said openly that he had only one wish: "Reduce all Christian empires to nothing"

In the Hagia Sophia the Turks built this raised seat for the sultans to attend prayers while being separated from the congregation

Iran

The Seljuk Turks had been in the Iranian province of Khurasan since the eleventh century. They had conquered much of Iran and Iraq under Togrul Beg, protector of the Sunni caliph of Baghdad. Iran had fallen to Mongols under Chingiz (Genghis) Khan and, in the 1400s, Timur. In 1534 Süleyman captured Tabriz and Baghdad, reestablishing Turkoman hegemony.

This would be overthrown by the Persian ruler Ismail I, who claimed descent from Ali, the fourth caliph. He had founded the Safavid dynasty in 1501. (It lasted until 1736.) It was Ismail who established the Shiah doctrine as Iran's state religion and began a century of conflict with the Sunni Ottomans.

Ottoman Administration

Süleyman was called "the Magnificent" abroad. At home he was called "the Just" or *Kanuni* (the Lawgiver) because of his modifications to the legal system of Mehmed II. How much of this was flattery is difficult to ascertain. Certainly the sultan controlled all power in his own court. He had a very personal style of government. Although he had two sons killed for arguing with him, Roxelana, one of his wives, was a trusted advisor. In Istanbul he established a shelter for sick or disabled Janissaries. The sultan himself served in the first battalion of the corps.

The system that Süleyman I established for his enormous empire was comprehensive

Süleyman won his greatest victory near Mohács in 1526, where he defeated the Hungarian cavalry

Areas occupied by the different Ottoman emperors from 1350 to 1560

1564

Selim imperii potitus

Selim I reigned from 1512 to 1520. Etching by Gaspar Bouttats

enough to keep the Turkish Empire intact for three hundred years. Its various institutions, particularly under Mehmed II, had been developing for at least that long. Like Sultan Mehmed II and all devout Muslims, he considered the Koran to have been written by God and revealed to the Prophet Muhammad. Hence, its words were infallible and meant to be interpreted literally. *Sunna* (the conduct of the Prophet Muhammad) provided the example to be followed.

Socially, the empire had two classes, the Ottomans and a class of people called *rayas* (protected flock). The higher class comprised a Muslim aristocracy (which included Turks, Persians, and Arabs) and Christian prisoners and slaves. The Christians were recruited, converted, and educated through a system called *devshirme* throughout the sixteenth century. During Süleyman's reign, the devshirme recruits achieved control, driving the Turkish aristocracy out of the ruling class and exploiting the state to their own advantage.

The sultan had total authority over imperial resources. He acquired huge estates from the rulers he vanquished in the course of his conquests. He leased these to his followers, Turkish vassals with essentially no political power. Under the Islamic laws of inheritance, women were not permitted to come into possession of land. When a family of vassals died out, the estates reverted to the sultan.

The government was organized by function into four branches or institutions. The Imperial Institution had an Inner Service to deal with palace matters and an Outer Service with a regulatory function. The Military Institution, led by the Janissaries and the cavalry, functioned in war, defense, and conquest.

Under the Scribal Institution, Süleyman established twenty-one virtually independent provinces. These, in turn, were divided into 250 *sanchaks*, or administrative districts organized for financial purpose. The districts were run by slaves, agents of the sultan accorded the social status of their master. Given the authority to collect taxes, they acted as an administrative civil service. The payment of *zakat* (an alms-giving tax) was required of all Muslims, especially the wealthy. Intended to help the poor, particularly in health care and education, tax revenues also went to pay the ransoms of captives, the costs of *jihad* (holy war), and conversion inducements to Islam.

The Religious Institution provided Muslim guidance, education, and the administration of justice. *Islam* is the Arabic word for "surrender." Islamic law and ethics, called *Sharia*, assumed a willingness to surrender to the will of Allah and to carry out social obligations. Süleyman did not insist on universal conversion to Islam. At least twenty different peoples inhabited the empire. The sultan tolerated them all, leaving them free to practice their devotions as long as they paid extra poll tax *(jizyah)*. They were organized into *millets* (communities) under their own leaders who acquired greater importance under Turkish authority than they would have achieved on their own. They included Jews and Christians of varied persuasion (Greek and Bulgarian Orthodox, Armenian Gregorian, and Roman Catholic).

With the advent of the nineteenth century, the Ottoman Empire declined. As the sultans weakened, people in prosperous western Europe spoke of the "sick man on the Bosporus." Nevertheless, Süleyman's successors continued to pose a threat. Vienna was besieged after 1529 as well.

The fortifications on the island of Rhodes. The islanders defended themselves successfully against a siege by Mehmed II, but were defeated by Süleyman the Magnificent.

1566

TIME LINE

	PRE–COLUMBIAN CULTURE POLITICS	**PRE–COLUMBIAN CULTURE CULTURAL HISTORY**	**EVENTS IN THE REST OF THE WORLD**
BC 30,000	**c.30,000–20,000** First groups of hunters migrate from North to South America **c.17,000** Traces of the first settlements in South America		
1300	**c.2000–AD 300** Preclassical Maya civilization **c.1300/1200 BC–AD 200** Olmec civilization on the Caribbean coast	**1300/1200–200** Olmec civilization develops, characterized by hierarchical structure; cultivation of maize; hunting and fishing; jaguar viewed as creator of man	
1000			
900	**c.900 BC** Rise of the Chimú civilization in South America **c.600** Foundation of Teotihuacán as a group of small villages **c.300** Rise of theTiwanaku (Tihuanaco) civilization **c.200** Teotihuacán becomes a city	**c.900–500** Maya live as nomads; build small villages; cultivate maize; population increases **c.900–AD 300** Evolution of the ball game *ulama*; use of slash-and-burn method of agriculture	
200 **AD** 100		**c.100** Construction of the Pyramid of the Sun in Teotihuacán **150** Peak of Teotihuacán culture; extensive commercial ties	
200	**c.150** Teotihuacán becomes a state; its power reaches Mayan territory		
300	**c.300** Collapse of the Preclassical Mayan Empire caused by political crisis **c.300–900** Beginning of Classical Maya culture in the Yucatán	**c.300** Maya have calendars, astronomy, network of cities, city-states ruled by the elite **c.300–900** Maya write in glyphs **c.300–1200** Tiwanaku (Tihuanaco) becomes major power on the Altiplano, its region influenced by the Incas	**c.220** Chinese Buddhism develops
400			
500	**c.500** Internal fighting among the Maya, city-states' elite want more power	**c.500** Urbanization and rapid population growth of the Maya **c.500** Maya cities reinforced with walls; construct stone buildings; form professional groups	
600			
700	**c.750** End of Teotihuacán **c.750–900** No dominant culture in Central America; various migrations through the Valley of Mexico		**618** Tang dynasty begins in China **732** Battle of Poitiers (France); Charles Martel defeats the Muslims
800	**c.800** Rise of the Chibcha civilization in South; Classical Maya culture collapses	**c.800–1300** Chibchas develop high-level gold processing	**800** Charlemagne crowned emperor of Holy Roman Empire
900	**c.900** Beginning of the Toltec Empire and foundation of Tula; rise of independent Maya city-states	**c.950** High point of the Toltec culture	
1000			**955** Emperor Otto I defeats the Magyars at Lechfeld **969** Conquest of Egypt by the Fatimids **1014** Basil II of Byzantium defeats the Persians **1066** Battle of Hastings (England)
1100	**c.1150** End of the Toltec Empire; Tula is abandoned; the Mexica move south **c.1150–1345** Various peoples (including the Mexica) settle in the Valley of Mexico, power struggles ensue		**1185** First shogunate in Japan **1202–1204** Fourth Crusade; Crusaders capture Byzantium **1215** Magna Carta in England **1227** Death of Chingiz (Genghis) Khan **1235** First Bulgarian patriarchate **1250–1275** Marco Polo travels through China
1200	**c.1250** The Mexica settle near Lake Texcoco as tributaries of the Tepanecs; first Inca kings	**c.1250** The Mexica subsist on agriculture, population increases	

Prehistory	Antiquity	Middle Ages	Renaissance	Modern History	Contemporary History

	PRE–COLUMBIAN CULTURE POLITICS	PRE–COLUMBIAN CULTURE CULTURAL HISTORY	EVENTS IN THE REST OF THE WORLD
1300		c.1300 Incas live around the city of Cuzco as simple peasants	1307 Beginning of the Babylonian exile of the popes; flowering of the Mali Empire
			1337 Advent of the Hundred Years' War in Europe
1350	1345 Tenochtitlán founded 1345–1445 The Mexica enter into alliance with the cities of Texcoco and Tlacopan against the Tepanecs	c.1345 The Mexica found the city of Tenochtitlán, become dominating power of alliance called Aztec	1350 Black Death in Europe 1360 Flowering of the Mongol Empire under Timur (Tamerlane)
1400	1400–1500 Weak Mayan alliance at Mayapán c.1430 Beginning of the expansion of the Inca Empire under Viracocha; conquest of the area around Lake Titicaca 1438 Chanca invade the Inca Empire and attack Cuzco; Viracocha picks Urqon as successor; Cusi Yupanqui defeats the Chanca and conquers new regions 1438–1471 Panchacuti (Pachacuti) Inca Yupanqui rules the Incas 1445 Tenochtitlán becomes the capital of the Aztec Empire		1429 Joan of Arc ends the siege of Orléans
		c.1445 Aztec society organized into multiple ranks; state is divided into administrative units c.1450 Incan society forms tribes; divides into four provinces 1458 Aztecs go to war seeking wealth and victims for human sacrifice	
1450	1458 Aztecs, under Motecuhzoma I (Montezuma) begin conquest of Mixtec territory 1462–1470 Incas conquer the Chimú Empire 1469 Death of Motecuhzoma I (Montezuma); succeeded by Axayácatl		1449 Unity restored in the Christian Church 1453 First Europeans in Japan 1462 Ivan III the Great, first czar of Russia
	1481–1486 Tizoc rules the Aztec Empire 1486 Ahuitzotl becomes ruler of the Aztecs and conquers northern coast	1487 Four thousand people sacrificed by Ahuitzotl to celebrate expansion of the temple to Huitzilopochtli	
1500	1492 Columbus arrives at islands off South America 1493 Huayna Capac conquers parts of the Andes and Ecuador	1493–1525 Royal seat of the Incas moved from Cuzco to Tumibamba	1498 Vasco da Gama reaches southern India
	1502 Motecuhzoma II (Montezuma II) succeeds Ahuitzotl as Aztec ruler 1519/1532 Spaniards land in Central and South America 1519–1521 Under Hernán Cortés, Spaniards destroy the Aztec Empire 1525 Brotherly feud divides the Inca Empire 1525–1532 Huscar rules the Inca Empire 1532 Francisco Pizarro disrupts the Inca Empire with Spanish troops, takes Inca king prisoner 1533 Atahuallpa executed by Spanish troops	1520 European diseases weaken the Incas	1520 Süleyman II the Great becomes ruler of the Ottomans
1550		c.1550 Postconquest recording of *Popol Vuh* myth	

	CHINA POLITICAL HISTORY	CHINA CULTURAL HISTORY	EVENTS IN THE REST OF THE WORLD
BC **390**		386 BC Foundation of the Hung secret society	
200	206 BC–AD 220 Han dynasty; restoration of the empire under General Liu Pang		
150	150 BC Threat of the Hsiung–nu from the north		
140	140–86 Emperor Wu Ti leads the Chinese Empire to its peak	145–97 BC Historian Ssu–ma Ch'ien 140–86 BC Construction of fortresses and fortifications against the Huns	
120	c.121 China conquers the Tarim Basin		
100		c.100 BC Silk trade with Greece	

Prehistory	Antiquity	Middle Ages	Renaissance	Modern History	Contemporary History

1568

AD	CHINA POLITICAL HISTORY	CHINA CULTURAL HISTORY	EVENTS IN THE REST OF THE WORLD
0	**9** Wang Mang ascends throne; beginning of the Hsin dynasty **22** End of Wang Mang control; restoration of the Han dynasty; anarchy and revolts		
100		**92** Death of historian Pan-ku **100** Silk trade with the Roman Empire **105** Tsai-lun invents paper	**150** Teotihuacán becomes a genuine state
200		**c.200** Introduction of the Mandarin examination; tax reform	
	c.220–265/280 Chinese Empire breaks into three states; war and confusion; invasions by Mongols and the Hsiung–nu	**c.220–280** Buddhist monks settle in China; emergence of Chinese Buddhism **c.225** Confucianism becomes state religion	
	263 End of the Shu Empire **265** End of the Wei Empire **280** End of the Wu Empire **c.306** Rise of the Chin dynasty in the east **316–589** Six dynasties fight for power	**316–589** Flowering of astronomy, mathematics, chemistry, biology, trade	
300			
400			
500	**c.420** Chin dynasty succeeded by Liu Sung dynasty; Wei Empire of the Tartars develops in the north **589** General Yang Chien becomes emperor **589–618** Sui dynasty from the north conquers the south	**589** Building of the Grand Canal, rebuilding of the Great Wall, reforms in national government and penal code	
600			
	c.618 Under Kao–tsu, China becomes the world's greatest empire, bureaucracy streamlined **618–907** Tang dynasty		**618–900** Korea and Japan influenced by Chinese civilization
700	**712–756** Chinese Empire in difficulty, Emperor Ming-huang introduces tax reform **c.750** China conflicts with the emerging power of Islam	**c.700** Foundation of Han-li academy, revival of Confucianism **c.750** Invention of the printing press, flowering of poetry **c.800** Introduction of paper money	
800	**c.800–907** Breakup of the Tang dynasty; bandits terrorize the countryside; empire breaks down into states		**800** Charlemagne crowned emperor of Holy Roman Empire
900	**c.960** General Zhao Kuangyin acclaimed; conquers the south **960–1279** Sung dynasty	**960** Order and peace restored; trade increases; China regains prosperity; growth of cities; population increase fosters crisis	**969** Fatimids conquer Egypt **1001** Mahmud of Ghazni occupies the Punjab (India)
1000	**c.1000–1100** Pressure on the empire's borders	**c.1025** Hang Zhou has more than one million inhabitants **c.1050** Foundation of charity institutions in the cities	
1100	**c.1125** Juchen founds the Chin dynasty, conquers the Sung capital and takes the emperor prisoner **1125–1279** Beginning of the Sung dynasty in the south **1227** Death of Chingiz (Genghis) Khan **1235** Kublai Khan becomes sole ruler of the Chin Empire		**c.1150** End of the Toltec Empire **1185** First shogunate of Japan **1204** Byzantium captured by the Crusaders
1200		**1246** Mongols found Beijing as new capital in the north **c.1250–1275** Venetian Marco Polo travels through China **c.1250–1350** Pax Mongolia **1267** Construction of Beijing completed	**c.1250** The Mexica settle near Lake Texcoco
	1271 Mongol dynasty becomes the Yüan dynasty **1279** Mongols rule all of China **1294** Death of Kublai Khan		**1301** Osman I founds the Ottoman Empire **1310** Most of India under Muslim domination of the Tughlug dynasty **1345** The Mexica found the city of Tenochtitlán **1360** Timur (Tamerlane) leads Mongol Empire to its peak **1462** Ivan III the Great proclaims himself czar of Russia
1300			
1400	**1368** Beginning of the Ming dynasty		

Prehistory	Antiquity	Middle Ages	Renaissance	Modern History	Contemporary History

THE FIRST RUSSIAN PRINCIPALITIES POLITICAL HISTORY	THE FIRST RUSSIAN PRINCIPALITIES CULTURAL HISTORY	EVENTS IN THE REST OF THE WORLD
900		
	899 Vladimir and his court are baptized Orthodox Christian; forced conversion of the Russian people; construction of churches and monasteries	
950	**c.950** Swedes reach Byzantium's capital via the Russian steppes	
		969 Fatimids conquer Egypt
978–1005 Vladimir I rules Kyyiv (Kiev) Empire		**1001** Mahmud of Ghazni occupies the Punjab
1000	**c.1000** Cultural influences from Byzantium, Judaism, and Islam	
1015–1019 Battles over succession to Vladimir	**1015** Vladimir canonized	
1019–1054 Yaroslav assumes power; Great Russian Empire emerges, maintained through oppression		
1050 **1054** Yaroslav dies; empire divides into principalities	**1050** Kyyiv becomes trade center	
		1066 Battle of Hastings
1100 **c.1100** Boyars become important influence on ruler; central authority weakens	**c.1100** Boyars own most land, employ serfs to work it	
1200		**1122** Concordat of Worms (England)
		c.1150 End of the Toltec Empire
1223 Mongol victory over the Russians at Kalka		**1227** Death of Chingiz (Genghis) Khan
		1235 Kublai Khan becomes sole ruler of Chinese Empire
1240 Mongols raze Kyyiv; Novgorod pays tribute to survive	**c.1240** Moscow becomes center of Orthodox Christian culture in Russia, welcomes refugees	
1245 Empire of the Golden Horde; Mongols hold sway in Russia		
1250 **c.1250** Mongols grant Moscow ruler the title "Grand Duke"	**c.1250–1480** Cultural stagnation in Russia under Mongol rule	**1250** Venetian Marco Polo travels to China
c.1250–1480 High tribute paid by Russian princes		
1300		**1316–1341** Lithuania conquers the Ukraine
1350 **c.1350** The grand dukes of Moscow increase their autonomy		**1337** Start of the Hundred Years' War (Europe)
1380 Battle of Kulikovo, Russian army defeats the Mongol Horde, Moscow takes lead among Russian states		**1360** Timur (Tamerlane) leads the Mongol Empire to its peak
1400	**c.1390** The Russian Church secedes from Eastern Church	
1450	**1453** Moscow considers itself the Third Rome	**1453** Byzantium captured by the Ottoman Turks
1462 Ivan III considers himself rightful heir to the Byzantine basilicus	**1462** Russian rulers take the title *czar*	
1462–1505 Ivan III the Great keeps Lithuanians and Mongols under control and conquers Novgorod		
1500 **1494** Ivan III confiscates all property of the merchants of Novgorod, reducing it to a provincial town		
		1519 Spaniards land in Central America
		1520 Süleyman II the Great rules the Ottomans

Prehistory	Antiquity	Middle Ages	Renaissance	Modern History	Contemporary History

AFRICA POLITICAL HISTORY	AFRICA CULTURAL HISTORY	EVENTS IN THE REST OF THE WORLD
1050 Mande people found a small state along the Niger		
1056 Ibn Yassin dies, succeeded by Abū Bakr		
c.1066 Ghana is the most powerful state in the Sudan, government by absolutist monarchy	**1066** Gold exports bring Ghana great power	**1066** Battle of Hastings (England)
1076 The Ghanese Empire is plundered by the Almoravids		
		1122 Concordat of Worms (England)
1203–1204 Susu king discovers the power of small Mali		**1204** Conquest of Byzantium by the Crusaders
		1227 Death of Chingiz (Genghis) Khan
1235 Sundiata founds the Mali Empire, after defeating the Susu king	**1235** Introduction of cotton cultivation and textile manufacture in Mali	
1240 Sundiata destroys the old city of Ghana		**1250–1275** Marco Polo travels through Venetian China
1307–1332 Golden Age of the Mali Empire under Congo Mansu; conquest of Timbuktu and Gao	**1307–1332** Pilgrimage of Congo Mansu to Mecca; construction of the mosque of Gao	**1310** Muslim Tughluq dynasty dominates India
	c.1350 Ibn Battuta of Tangier describes the Mali kingdom	
		1380 Russians defeat the Mongol horde
1433 Timbuktu conquered by the Tuareg		**1453** Ottoman Turks cause the fall of Byzantium
		1462 Ivan III the Great, czar of Russia
1465–1492 Sonni Ali rules the Songhai Empire		
1473 Jenné vanquished by the Songhai		
1493 General Askia Mamadou Toure stages coup d'etat in Songhai; western Sudan reunited		
c.1500 Askia develops an efficient government	**c.1500** Jenné, Walata, Gao, and Timbuktu grow into famous university cities; Leo Africanus, *The History and Description of Africa*	
1513 Conquest of the Hausa states by Askia		
	1519 Mahmud Kati, *Tarikh el fettach*	**1519–1532** Spaniards land in Central America
1528 Abdication ends the regime of Askia		**1520–1566** Süleyman I the Great rules the Ottomans
1542 Death of Askia		
1590 Gao conquered by Moroccan armies		
c.1700 Bambara found Segu and Kaarta		
1810 Jenné occupied by Bambara; Fulani defeat Bambara		
1893 French reach Jenné		

Prehistory	Antiquity	Middle Ages	Renaissance	Modern History	Contemporary History

	JAPAN POLITICAL HISTORY	JAPAN CULTURAL HISTORY	EVENTS IN THE REST OF THE WORLD
BC 200,000	**c.200,000–10,500** First people in Japan **10,500–400 BC** Jomōn culture **660** Legendary foundation of Japan by Emperor Jimmu Tenno	**200,000–250** Society comprises hunters, gatherers, and fishermen	
400	**400–AD 250** Yayoi culture; migration to Japan from China	**400–AD 250** Cultivation of rice; increased population; migrations into Japan via Korea	
AD 250	**AD 250** Local political unity; Land of the Queens, according to Chinese histories	**AD 250–600** Funeral practices include burial mounds and gifts	
300	**300** Kofun culture centered in Kinai region; first Japanese invasion of Korea; Japanese kings hold military supremacy in Korea	**AD 300** Kyushu attains high level of civilization; fearsome cavalry	
400		**c.400** Sun cult becomes national religion; Koreans hold prominent court positions as advisors	
450	**c.450** Yamato Empire begins; incipient court system		
500			
	538 Emperor accepts Buddhism **592** Umako, leader of the Soga clan, has the emperor assassinated **593–622** Shotoku Taishi introduces a system of government based on Chinese model	**538** Introduction of Buddhism; Chinese and Korean influences **593–622** Expansion of Buddhism	
600	**600–710** Asuka period **622** Soga clan returns to traditional politics **645–710** End of political supremacy of the Soga clan; beginning of the Taika period of political reform; Emperor Kotoku is absolute ruler	**c.600** Writing of history begins in Japan **646** Farmers become free leaseholders; no private ownership of land	**AD 618** Beginning of the Tang dynasty in China
700	**710–794** Nara period	**c.700** Residential capitals **710** Empress Gemmyo starts building the capital of Nara **712** *Record of Ancient Matters* (Kojiki) **720** First written history of Japan, *The Chronicles of Japan* (Nikon Shoki)	
800	**794–1185** Heian period; Kyoto becomes capital **858–1160** Fujiwara family controls central government	**858–1160** Overpopulation; conflicts with the Ainu; origin of Japanese script; reintroduction of death penalty; large standing army	**800** Charlemagne crowned emperor
900			
1000	**c.1000–1100** Crisis in the empire; imperial treasury empty	**c.1000** *The Tale of Genji*, world's first novel, written by court lady-in-waiting Murasaki Shikobu	
1100	**1068** Emperor Go-Sanjo confiscates large landed estates **1100** Fujiwara ended as political power **1156** Warriors occupy Kyoto; beginning of civil wars **1160–1185** Taira clan controls central government **1185** Minamoto family takes power under Yoritomo; first shogunate established in Kamakura **1185–1333** Kamakura period	**1185** Country is ravaged as the result of civil war	**1066** Battle of Hastings
1200	**1266** Emissary of Kublai Khan demands subjugation **1274** First Mongol attack **1281** Second Mongol attack, repelled by typhoon, the legendary "Divine Wind"		**1227** Death of Chingiz (Genghis) Khan **1235** Kublai Khan ruler of the Chin Empire **1279** The Mongols rule China
1300	**1331** Emperor tries to abolish shoguns **1333** Emperor Go-Daigo comes to power **1333–1573** Ashikaga or Moromachi period **1336–1392** Yoshino period **1338** Takauji deposes emperor and becomes shogun **1392** Court reunited	**c.1300** Feudal large landowners control the countryside	**1301** Osman I founds the Ottoman Empire **1310** Tughlug Muslim dynasty dominates India **c.1350** Outbreak of bubonic plague (Black Death) in Europe
1400		**c.1400** Ashikaga support for arts, flowering of Zen	**1453** Ottoman Turks conquer Byzantium **1532** Spanish troops disrupt the Inca Empire
1500	**1467–1568** Period of the Warring States **1543** First Europeans in Japan **1573** Last Ashikaga shogun deposed	**1467–1568** Civil war destroys many temples and private collections of art **1573–1615** Momoyama period in the arts	

Prehistory	Antiquity	Middle Ages	Renaissance	Modern History	Contemporary History

Glossary

administered trade heavily taxed trade strictly regulated by traditional African monarchs, to increase power of the ruling classes.

acllas daughters of the Inca nobility chosen to spend their lives between the ages of eight and sixteen in a convent serving the king; some were sacrificed, while others became Inti priestesses or were married to yaconas.

African states states developed between 800 BC and AD 1000 that were often characterized by social inequality and political friction; trade was controlled by the ruling class.

Ashikaga period (1338–1573) period during which the noble family of Ashikaga ruled Japan; after ousting emperor Go-Daigo (1333–1338), they conquered the shogunate.

Askia Mamadu Ture general and ruler of the Songhai Empire (1493–1528); he introduced Islam as a state religion.

ayllu a small extended family in the Inca Empire, a landholding unit with social and administrative functions.

Aztec Empire pre-Columbian state in Central America that subjugated the Huastec to the north and the Mixtec and Zapotec to the south; under Motecuhzoma I (c. AD 1468) territory was won from the Mixteca; a composite civilization developed, based on Mixteca-Puebla heritage; agriculture and trade flourished; between AD 1519 and 1521 the Spaniards, under the leadership of Hernán Cortés, conquered the empire.

Aztec religion belief in a variety of gods with the ability to change character, who were worshiped with human sacrifices; the sun-god, Tonatiuh, and the earth monster, a devouring and nurturing goddess, were dual figures in this society; Tlaloc, the rain god and Huitzilopochtli, the war god, were among the several other gods.

Aztecs pre-Columbian culture in the Mexican Valley, established by nomads and Mexica who founded the Aztec Empire in the fifteenth century, with Tenotitlán as its primary city; engineering, architecture, art, mathematics, astronomy, sculpture, weaving, metalwork, music, and picture writing were advanced Aztec developments.

Bajezid Lightning (c.1360–1402) (also known as Bayezid or Bajazet I, Thunderbolt) first Osman ruler to be given title of sultan; put down Balkan revolt, besieged Constantinople; in 1402 he was captured by the Mongols under Tamerlane (Timurlenk), and exhibited in a cage.

Battle at Varna (1444) battle between an Osman army and a Polish-Hungarian army, during which the Christian army was slaughtered; this crusade had been called by the pope to counteract the successful Turkish conquests in the Balkans and Asia Minor.

bojars Russian noblemen, major landowners whose feudal power had a detrimental effect on Kyyiv's (Kiev) central rule.

Byzantium ancient city of Thrace, founded by the Greeks in 667 BC, selected by Constantine I as the site for Constantinople in AD 330; later it served as the capital of the Byzantine Empire; known as Istanbul after the Turkish defeat.

calpixque Aztec official responsible for paying tribute owed to Tlatoani.

calpullis administrative units in the Aztec Empire drawn from a group of related families; each calpulli was given a plot of land to farm, a temple, and a school and, in turn, supplied soldiers and labor for public works.

camayos social groups in Inca society, comprising craftsmen, farmers, soldiers, and traders who devoted their services to the king; they were exempt from military service.

capacochas ten-year-olds offered to the gods on the Inca altars at Cuzco; after death they were worshiped as divinities.

Chibcha (Muisca) pre-Columbian culture in the South American Andes first established c.300 BC, existing to the sixteenth century AD; their two tribes, Zipas and Zaques, were divided into leaders and priests, people and slaves; they offered slaves to the sun-god.

Chimú people who developed an ancient civilization on the desert coast of northern Peru that flourished after c.1200; used irrigation to turn desert land into fertile farming land, and had a complex social system and a well-planned capital, Chan Chan; surrendered to the Inca Empire c.1460.

Chin non-Chinese dynasty that ruled an empire in northern China (1115–1234); concluded a treaty with the Sung from the north against the Mongolian nomads, the Liao; in 1125 they forced the Sung to move south.

chinampas agricultural land skirted by trees to protect the raised soil from erosion; corn and beans were the first crops cultivated.

Chinese historiography first introduced by Ssu-ma (145–97 BC) and continued by Pan-ku (c. AD 92); Ssu-ma divided all narrations into components: the emperor; organization of the empire; culture, geography and economics; and biographies.

Chingiz Khan (Genghis Khan) Mongolian ruler (1167–1227); in 1190 he united the Mongols and was recognized as the great khan by the Kurultai (meeting of clan chiefs); established a Mongolian world empire by conquering China and some Islamic empires.

Chola early kingdom and maritime power, founded by former vassals, comprising much of southeast India, Kerala, Mysore, and Ceylon (Sri Lanka); kingdom existed from fourth century BC.

Cuzco capital of the Inca Empire, Tahuantinsuyu, located primarily in present-day Peru, founded by the legendary king Manco Capac; center for religion, temples, altars, and sacrificial offerings of capacochas.

daimyo Japanese class of landowners, originally farmer leaders of humble origin, who introduced an efficient government of land and vassals; class developed during Period of Warring States.

Dekkhan area in southern India ruled from sixth to the eighth centuries by the Chalukyo dynasty; Pulakesin II (608–642) expanded the region; Rashtrakutra dynasty (757–1190) was brought down by Muslim aggression.

Djenné town in the inner delta of the Niger River, famous for its clay architecture and peaceful society built around a variety of cultures; Djenné belonged to Mali and was conquered in 1473 by the Songhai.

Empire of the Golden Horde Mongolian empire comprising most of Russia whose name derives from its capital, the Mongol camp on the Volga; separated in 1240 from the Mongols in the east, it exploited Russian principalities by extracting annual taxes; internal warfare and attempts by Russian princes to end payment of taxes weakened the empire, and Tamerlane (Timurlenk) defeated it in the late fourteenth century.

flower wars fought for economic reasons and to expand land; prisoners of war were sacrificed to the Aztec gods during the many religious celebrations.

Fujiwara period (858–1160) period in which the Fujiwara-uji were the actual controlling power in Japan; they filled the offices of Sesshu, the emperor's regent, and Kampaku, head of civil authority; increasing power of the army diminished their control.

Genghis Khan See Chingiz Khan.

Ghana West African empire established in the eighth century AD that dominated the savanna region around the year 1050; Soninke were the Islamic ruling class and they controlled the gold trade and endorsed organized commercial traffic in Africa; Ghana collapsed around 1200 under the emergence of other western African states; modern Ghana takes its name from the ancient empire.

Great Moguls Mongolian Muslim dynasty established under Babur Shah (1526–1530) in India; authority of the Great Moguls extended to India, but diminished in the eighteenth century.

Gupta Empire Indian dynasty (c.320–c.544) that ruled much of what is now modern India; brought down by the invasions of the White Huns; leading monarchs were Samudra Gupta (335–375), who made extensive conquests, and Chandra Gupta II (375–414).

Han dynasty dynasty in control of China (206 BC–AD 221); restored the agrarian economy and introduced Confucianism as the state religion; defeated the Huns and undertook expeditions across the Chinese

1573

borders; government tasks were fulfilled by state officials from the class of large landowners called mandarins.

Harsha Buddhist leader heading an empire (606–647) in northern India comprising parts of the former Gupta Empire.

heys title of high officials in the Osman Empire; they collected taxes in the provinces and recruited warriors.

huacas sacred objects of the Inca religion; objects, places, altars, and persons could be worshiped as huacas or were sometimes used as oracles; Incas would also worship as huacas the religious elements of conquered peoples.

Hulaku brother of the Mongolian rulers Mangu (1251–1260) and Kublai Khan (1260–1294), who conquered Baghdad, Aleppo, and Damascus; when Kublai Khan became chief khan, Hulaku officially recognized him, but continued to rule the Mongols in the west.

Inca Viracocha (c. AD 1438) king of the Incas in the fifteenth century and first to conquer land outside Inca territory; his successors, Pachacuti, Tupac Yupanqui, and Huayna Capac, expanded the Inca Empire by conquering in north and south.

Inca Empire (Tahuantinsuyu) pre-Columbian empire from the thirteenth century to 1532, stretching from the northern parts of Ecuador south to Argentina; fifteenth century saw a rapid expansion of the empire; conquered in 1532 by Pizarro.

Inca religion religion based on worship of a universal deity possessing a multitude of divine powers and personalities; personages of this one god included Viracocha, the creator, and Inti, the sun-god and the kings' forefather; Incas also worshiped their forefathers, their kings, huacas, and capacochas.

Incas pre-Columbian civilization in South America that established the Inca Empire in the thirteenth century; they were an expansionist society controlled by a king; people lived in groups called ayllus and provided services to the state in the form of military service and labor on roads, buildings, and state-controlled farms; textiles were used for clothing but also were a status symbol.

Indian trade India traded with Rome, Persia, Greece, the Arab realm, and China; was a transit center for trade (including silk) with China and exported spices, precious stones, animals, and textiles; commercial trade spread Hinduism and Buddhism, Indian philosophy, and science.

Ivan III the Great grand duke of Muscovy (1462–1505); subdued the Mongols and Lithuanians; after the fall of Constantinople, Muscovy was all that remained of the Christian Byzantine Empire, and Ivan took on the role of emperor over this reduced territory and established the Russian Czarist Empire; the word *Czar* is a Slavic word meaning "Caesar," or "Emperor."

1574 **Janizaries** (also Janissaries) army of slaves

and Christian prisoners of war who were indoctrinated with Turkish culture and military discipline; they stood as the basis for the military successes the Turks enjoyed between 1360 and 1826; regular outbreaks of janizary revolts took place from the seventeenth century onward; their power ended in 1826 when Sultan Mahmud II had them massacred in their barracks.

Kamakura period (1192–1333) period in which Japan was ruled by shoguns of the Minamoto-uji (later followed by other clans) from Kamakura; the Minamoto defeated the Taira after a power struggle and Yoritomo Minamoto became the first shogun.

Kanun Nam collection of Osman Turkish laws and regulations based on Islamic law and the absolute supremacy of the sultan, recorded in the fifteenth century by order of Muhammad II.

Kiev See Kyyiv.

Knights of St. John Christian Hospitalers who ruled the eastern parts of the Mediterranean from 1310 to 1522 from the island of Rhodes; in 1481 they withstood an Osman siege; when Rhodes was conquered (1522) they moved to a new stronghold on Malta in (1530).

Kojiki Japanese myth cycle centered around the creation of the world, including the narration of Jimmu Tenno, who established a Japanese state in the Yamato Plain in 660 BC; historians date this traditional first emperor to the third or fourth century AD.

Kublai Khan Mongol ruler (1260–1294); established the Yuan dynasty in Khan Baug (Peking); his court was a center for Chinese culture; conquered land in the Far East and appointed Chinese and Islamic officials.

Kyyiv (or Kiev) capital of the Russian empire of Vladimir and Yaroslav, who was formally in charge of the independent principalities after his death; Kyyiv was a flourishing trade center and seat of the Byzantine church; destroyed in 1240 by the Mongols.

Land of the Queens Chinese name for Japan at the time of the Tombe civilization, indicating the existence of a political unity around the year 300 and possibly a matriarchal society; also known under the name of Wa.

Latin America Central and South America as colonized by Latin people from Spain and Portugal from the sixteenth century onward; Spanish and Portuguese are now the main languages spoken in Latin America.

Lithuanians people to the north of Russia who conquered parts of Russia and the Ukraine in the fourteenth century; Ivan the Great managed to confine their expansion.

Machu Picchu it is believed to have sheltered the last acllas after the Spanish conquest.

Macehualtin Aztec farmers, craftsmen, and traders who paid tribute to the Tlatoani.

Mali Sudan kingdom established in the

eleventh century by the Mandinka along the Niger River; in the fourteenth century they controlled western Sudan and commercial traffic between Africa, Asia, and Europe; kingdom collapsed in the fifteenth century.

Marco Polo Venetian merchant (1254–1324) who stayed in the Far East (1271–1295) and worked as a minister for Kublai Khan; in 1298 he was taken prisoner by Genoa; he dictated his memoirs from his prison cell.

Maya cities built according to a fixed pattern: all cities had a central square that served as a marketplace, with temples, Ulama fields, palaces, graves, and water reservoirs; temples were large buildings situated on a terraced pyramid.

Maya elite religious, military, and political leaders who governed the city-states; as a demonstration of their power they made conquests and had the people, craftsmen, and farmers build stone buildings such as pyramids; family history and the worship of forefathers played an important role.

Maya religion the most important Maya gods, among the great many worshiped, were Hunapuh and Xbalanque, the Hero twins, while the Popul Vuh and the Ulama ball game fulfilled a central role; Mayas also worshiped their leaders, forefathers, and supernatural creatures.

Maya script ideographic script of illustrations and hieroglyphics with a phonetic value; although certain parts are still undeciphered, this is undoubtedly the most developed script of all Central American civilizations, and relates family history and historical events.

Mayas pre-Columbian civilization in Central America from 2000 BC to the present day; from 500 BC it changed to a society of city-states ruled by a Maya elite; great Maya realms could be found in Petén and Yucatán.

Mexica people from northern Mexico and creators of the Aztec Empire; after the fall of the Toltec Empire in the tenth century they settled in Texcoco and founded Tenochtitlán in 1345.

milpa agriculture Maya agricultural method whereby plots of rain forest were cultivated and left fallow after soil depletion, thus forcing the Mayas to move regularly; with the introduction of other farming methods, such as canalization, larger towns developed.

mitimas Inca subjects, both yanaconas and camayos, who were made to move from their original place of residence to work and live elsewhere.

Mongolian horde Mongolian army unit of 10,000 men set up by Chingiz (Genghis) Khan; army comprised separate units of ten men who would fight, hunt, and live together; hordes were all subject to the khan.

Mongolian religion Mongols practiced a monotheist religion inspired by the Nestorian Christians; they were never fully converted to Christianity; from the end of the thirteenth century the Mongols in the eastern parts of the empire were converted to Buddhism, western Mongols to Islam.

Mongols Asian tribes of horsemen to the north of China; Chingiz (Genghis) Khan united the Mongols in 1190 and became chief khan; in the twelfth and thirteenth centuries they conquered the Central Asian Islamic states, the sultanate of Delhi, Russia, China, and Japan.

Moscow (or Muscovy) Russian principality headed by a grand duke that became the seat of Byzantine Russian Christianity following the fall of Kyyiv (Kiev); Moscow separated from the Mongols in the late fourteenth century and stood at the head of all Russian principalities; after the conquest of Byzantium, Moscow became the new Christian center.

Mossi-Dagomba group African states and people who opposed the influence of Islam that was spread mainly by traders (djulas); they waged a guerrilla war against the Sudan Muslim states until the French occupation.

Muhammad of Ghur (?–1216) Muslim ruler who conquered an empire in northern India, where he ended the Delhi Hindu rule; his generals established the dynasty of Slave Kings and the Delhi sultanate.

Muslim from the Arabic, meaning one who surrenders to God; an adherent of Islam.

Neolithical Japanese civilizations the Jomōn civilization (2500–250 BC) possibly comprised hunters and gatherers from eastern Siberia; economy of the Yayoi civilization (250 BC–AD 250) in the south of Japan was based on rice farming; bronze, and later also iron, were used for symbolic and ritual purposes; Yayoi civilization disintegrated as the result of immigrants who brought with them iron weapons and tools.

Normanist school historical school positing the theory that the first Russian states were created by Scandinavian tribes.

Novgorod Russian trading post and manufacturing center for the German Hansa who monopolized trade in the North Sea and Baltic Sea; Novgorod came under Mongol threat in the thirteenth century; Ivan the Great conquered the city in 1471.

Ogodai Mongolian ruler (1229–1246); instructed his hordes to conquer Korea and the south of China and to raid Europe; after his death the Dnepr River became the far western border; assimilation of Mongols with the people they had overcome first started under his rule, and this led to the emergence of cultural differences.

Olmec pre-Columbian people in Central America on the Caribbean coast (1200 BC–AD 300), famous for its gigantic stone sculptures of heads and delicate jade objects; jaguar figure appears to have played an important role in Olmec religion.

Osman Turks Turks under the dynasty of the Osmans who established the Osman (Ottoman) Empire in 1300 in Asia Minor (1300–1922); they fought the Serbs, Mongols, Christians, and Persians and conquered parts of Europe, the Balkans, and the Middle East.

Pachacuti-Inca (Cusi Yupanqui) king of Incas (1438–1471); drove out the raiding Chancas and conquered their territory to the north of Cuzco.

Pala dynasty Buddhist dynasty controlling an empire from the eighth to the twelfth centuries in the Bengal region in northeastern India; Senas then took power, but they in turn were subjected by the Muslims.

Pallavas dynasty in southeast India from 500 to 800 that controlled the Hindu Tamils from the Dravida civilization; mostly followers of Buddhism and Brahmanism.

paper writing material invented by Tsai-lun in AD 105, made from rags and plant fiber; was introduced to the Arab world in the eighth century by Chinese prisoners of war; from there it spread to other parts of Europe; like silk, paper became an important export product.

paqana male descendants of deceased Sapa Inca who controlled the ayllu; according to ayllu tradition the authority and possessions of a deceased king would remain his; his worship would ensure the ayllu's fate after the Sapa's death.

Period of Warring States See Warring States period.

Petén region in Central America (Guatemala) where the Mayas lived in city-states in the Preclassical time (200 BC–AD 300); empire collapsed around 300, probably sparked by conflicts among the ruling classes; Mayas relocated to the Yucatán region.

pipiltin Aztec nobility comprising political advisors, governors, priests, and military leaders who supported the Tlatoani.

pochtecas a special class of traders in Aztec society who enjoyed a higher status, due to their economic importance and spying capacities in enemy territory.

Popul Vuh oral Maya version of the myth of the creation of the world; it was recorded in writing in the sixteenth century, depicting the nobility as semigods in order to enhance their position of power.

pre-Columbian age period preceding the discovery of America in 1492 and the Spanish and Portuguese colonization; Latin America was inhabited by different pre-Columbian civilizations, including the Mayas, Aztecs, and Incas; there is evidence for the first migrations at least 17,000 years ago, and the first settlements date from around 10,000 BC.

pre-Columbian civilization a collective name for multitude of civilizations living in Central and South America prior to fifteenth century invasions from European countries; primary among them are the Olmec, Maya, Teotihuacán, Inca, and Aztec.

printing first invented during the Tang dynasty, when texts were printed on paper using loose wooden letters; this encouraged the distribution of texts and made possible the first paper money notes.

private traders African trading class that developed under the influence of foreign trading posts established from the seventh century AD; private traders reorganized regional and local trade networks and laid the foundations for the Sudan kingdoms.

pyramid an architectural structure often of stone, having a rectangular base and four triangular sides; used as the foundation for temples and priest accommodations by many pre-Columbian societies, especially the Maya, Teotihuacán, and Aztec.

quipu pieces of knotted string used for administrative purposes in the Inca Empire; *quipucamayoc*, officials who knew how to arrange the knots, were in charge of such matters as recording public works and the distribution of excess food.

Rajputas warrior tribe in northwest India, with clans dominated by a military nobility; they are assumed to have arrived from the north as a marauding people; after 975 the empire disintegrated and was divided into states, to be finally defeated by the Muslims.

Red Eyebrows secret Chinese fellowship that established its authority in AD 8 under Wang Man and planned to introduce land reforms; their defeat by the Han fourteen years later ended in anarchy, which eventually brought down the Han dynasty.

Sahara desert region between North Africa and Sudan; the many commercial routes that ran through the region were controlled between 1000 and 1600 by Sudan kingdoms; introduction of the camel as a beast of burden encouraged the development of trade and the authority of the Sudan states.

Sapa Inca king of Incas, *Inca* being the title for Inca rulers; every ruler founded a new ayllu, for which he needed to conquer new territory and riches; he was worshiped after his death and continued his rule by way of the paqana.

Selim I Osman sultan (1512–1520) who planned to conquer the Muslim empires in the east; he conquered the Persian Empire and Syria and attacked the Mamelukes in Egypt; he appointed himself caliph.

Serbs central European Christian people who formed a strong state in the fourteenth century and posed a threat to the Osman Empire; they were defeated by the Osmans in 1389; Serb Empire was finally subjected in the late fifteenth century.

Shintoism indigenous Japanese religion based on the worship of forefathers; the sun goddess, Amaterasu, the first mother, was the most prominent of the goddesses; the emperor was revered as her leading priest and mythological son; Japan's national symbol became the rising sun.

shogun military Japanese commander, since 1192 the hereditary title of honor for the actual rulers of Japan; emperor was the virtual head of state; office continued to exist until 1868; shoguns belonged to the class of large landowners who exercised a feudal rule.

silk fine material made from the threads spun by the silkworm; this product was only produced in China, and Persian traders made huge profits on the silk trade; in 522 silkworm eggs were shipped to Byzantium and the Persian monopoly was opened up.

Six dynasties period in Chinese history (316–589) in which six dynasties fought for power; increased trade resulted in cultural and economic bloom; there were many Buddhist influences.

Slave Kings Muslim dynasty of the Delhi sultanate, an empire in northern India (1206–1526); its rulers tyrannized the Hindu population, leading to many revolts; their authority came under severe threat by Tamerlane's (Timurlenk) plundering raids in 1398 and they eventually lost it to the Great Moguls.

Sogas uji in the Yamato Empire who ruled Japan between 592 and 645 and who introduced Buddhism and related Chinese and Korean influences in technology, art, script, and philosophy; by introducing a Chinese hierarchy, Shotoku Taishi (573–622) planned to confine uji authority.

Soghai kingdom Sudan kingdom (1450–1540) centered around the capital of Gao, initially controlled by the Sunni dynasty and later, following a rebellion, by the Askia; Songhai controlled the Sahara's commercial routes, the salt mines, the tax system, and the commercial trade with northern Africa.

Süleyman I sultan of the Osman Empire (1520–1566); conquered Rhodes and Belgrade and controlled the Mediterranean, frustrating trade; reorganized the state and tolerated different religions in the empire.

Spaniards South European people who colonized Africa and conquered pre-Columbian civilizations in South and Central America; spread European diseases such as smallpox and influenza, thereby weakening the Incas, Mayas, and Aztecs.

Suche Bator (1893–1923) founder of the Mongolian People's Republic and leader of the Mongolian independence fighters during World War I; created a communist state in the Gobi Desert, the Mongolian ancestral land.

Sudan savanna region wedged between the Sahara and the tropical rain forests on the west coast; between 1000 and 1600 it saw the emergence of Islamic states that controlled the commercial routes through the Sahara and formed important trading posts for gold, salt, and trading with Asia and Europe.

sultan Islamic ruler of a Muslim state; rulers from the Osman state selected their successors from among their sons, who were then permitted to kill or lock up their brothers to prevent civil wars.

Sung dynasty dynasty that controlled China (960–1271); Sung Empire of the north (960–1125) was characterized by reinstate-ment of central authority, prosperity, and cultural bloom; were driven south by the Chin; Sung Empire of the south (1125–1271) quickly crumbled despite their use of gunpowder in weapons.

Taika reforms period of reforms in Japan (645–702) introduced by Emperor Kotoku, who became absolute ruler and landowner-ship was abolished; in 710 the construction of Nara was begun, which was to be Japan's capital until 794.

Tamerlane (Timurlenk) Mongolian ruler (1370–1405); around 1370 he subjected the Mongols in the west; conquered territory in Persia, India, Syria, and the Osman Empire and spread Islam; Mongolian power gradually disintegrated after his death.

Tang dynasty dynasty ruling China (618–907); arts and literature flowered during this period and Confucianism was reinstated; China became a world power through its conquests in Turkestan, Korea, Pomu, and Tibet; from the eighth century large landowners engaged in border conflicts and power struggles.

Tenochtitlán (Mexico City) capital of the Aztec Empire founded around AD 1345 by the Mexica; town boasted roads, a sewage system, water supply system, and a variety of temples; was divided into districts inhabited by people of the same profession and status.

Teotihuacán pre-Columbian society in Central America centered around their town of Teotihuacán from 600 BC to AD 750; around 200 BC Teotihuacán grew from a collection of villages to an influential city-state and economic center.

Three Kingdoms period in Chinese history (220–280) in which three kingdoms were in perfect balance: Wu (221–280), Wei in the north (221–265) and Shu in the southwest (221–263); chaotic period followed in 280, during which no ruling power emerged.

Tihuanaco pre-Columbian civilization that survived for several centuries from around 300 BC in the mountain regions of what is known today as Bolivia; a major temple is near Lake Titicaca; the Incas and others, were influenced by its religion.

Timurlenk See Tamerlane.

Tlatoani Aztec king chosen by the aristocracy from among the most eligible members of the royal family; candidates were healthy in body and mind and possessed knowledge of religious and military affairs.

Toltecs pre-Columbian empire in Central America centered around the city of Tula, north of present-day Mexico City, from the ninth until the twelfth centuries; their religion and architecture influenced other cultures, expecially the Aztecs.

Tombe civilization civilization (AD 300–800) in the Kinki region (China), characterized by enormous burial hills with symbols such as the magatama, or comma-shaped jewelry; it was possibly established by northeastern tribes of horsemen.

uji Japanese clans forming a tribal society worshiping their own god; the emperor stood at the head of all clans and political battles between clan leaders caused unrest.

ulama religious ball game organized by the Mayas; several playing fields have been discovered; intended for the nobility, the game's players symbolized themes from Maya religion; kings used the game to legitimize their power; losers often sacrificed.

ulemas Osman lawyers and consultants to the sultans and beys; they used their knowledge of the Turkish, Arab, and Persian languages and the Koran to consult the imperial government; also lectured on the Koran.

Vladimir I king of the Kyyivan (Kievan) Russian kingdom (980–1015); spread eastern Christianity in his kingdom to unite the many culturally diverse Slavic peoples; his son Yaroslav extended the kingdom from the Black Sea to the Gulf of Finland.

Warring States period period (1467–1568) in which the leading ujis fought for control; Ashikagas and Fujiwaras gradually lost their political power; revolts broke out against the feudalism of the Japanese landowners.

White Huns nomadic horsemen from Central Asia who raided India after 470 and brought down the Gupta Empire; empire later fell apart into small states; White Huns were driven from India around 500; they were also known as Heftakites.

Wu-ti ruler of the Han dynasty (140–86 BC) who reinforced China's position of power by entering into pacts with people from Central Asia and providing support against the Huns.

Yamato Empire uji empire controlled by the uji of the sun goddess, who made sun worship the state religion; controlled other Japanese ujis from the fifth century.

yanaconas social group within the Inca society; appointed from the aristocratic classes, they acted as personal assistants to the king and his noblemen; were released from the ayllu obligations of common citizens.

Yian dynasty Mongol dynasty established by Kublai Khan that ruled China (1271–1368); in 1368 the Chinese Ming dynasty subjected the Mongol Khans; Kublai Khan promoted the integration of Chinese and Mongol civilizations.

Yucatán region in Central America (Mexico) where the Mayas lived in city-states in the Classical period (300 BC–AD 900) and the Postclassical period (900–1500); Mayas fought many wars to expand their territory.

Bibliography

Pre-Columbian Cultures
Berrin and Pasztory. *Teotihuacán*. London, 1993.
Coe, M. D. *Mexico*. London, 1994.
Davies, N. *The Toltecs*. Norman, 1987.
Diehl and Berlo., eds. *Mesoamerica After the Decline of Teotihuacan*. Washington, 1989.
———. *Tula*. London, 1983.
Guthrie, J., ed. *The Olmec World*. Princeton, 1995.
Miller, M. E. *The Art of Mesoamerica from Olmec to Aztec*. London, 1986.
Sharer and Grove. *Regional Perspectives on the Olmecs*. Cambridge, 1989.

The Maya
Antochiw, M. *Route of the Mayas*. London, 1995.
Goetz and Morley. *Popol Vuh*. Norman, 1991.
MacAnay, P. A. *Living with the Ancestors*. Austin, 1995.
de Montmollin, O. *Settlement and Politics in Three Classic Maya Polities*. Madison, 1995.
Sabloff, J. A. *The New Archaeology and the Ancient Maya*. New York, 1994.
Sharer, R. J. *The Ancient Maya*. Stanford, 1994.
Taube, K. *Aztecs and Maya Myths*. Austin, 1993.
Wearne, P. *The Maya of Guatemala*. London, 1994.
Weaver, M. P. *The Aztecs, Maya and Their Predecessors*. San Diego, 1993.

The Aztecs
Bierhorst, J. *History and Mythology of the Aztecs*. Tucson, 1992.
Coe, M. D. *Mexico*. London, 1994.
Gillespie, S. D. *The Aztec Kings*. Tucson, 1989.
Glendinnen, I. *Aztecs*. Cambridge, 1991.
Grusinski, S. *The Aztecs: Rise and Fall of an Empire*. London, 1992.
Hassig, R. *Aztec Warfare*. Norman, 1988.
Hodge and Smiths. *Economies and Politics in the Aztec Realm*. Albany, NY, 1994.
Leon-Portilla, M. *The Broken Spears*. Boston, 1993.
Moctezuma, E. M. *The Aztecs*. New York, 1989.
———. *The Great Temple of the Aztecs*. London, 1994.
Taube, K. *Aztec and Maya Myth*. Austin, 1993.
Townsend, R. F. *The Aztecs*. London, 1992.
Weaver, M. P. *The Aztecs, Mayas and Their Predecessors*. San Diego, 1993.

The World of the Incas
Bauer, B. S. *The Development of the Inca State*. Austin, 1992.
Bauer and Dearborn. *Astronomy and Empire in the Ancient Andes*. Austin, 1992.
Cobe, B. *Inca Religion and Customs*. Austin, 1995.
Davies, N. *The Incas*. Niwat/Colorado, 1995.
Hemming, J. *The Conquest of the Incas*. London, 1993.
Kent, M. *Kinship and Labor in the Structure of the Inca Empire*. Michigan, 1989.

Malpass, M. A., ed. *Provincial Inca*. Iowa City, 1993.
Moseley, M. E. *The Incas and Their Ancestors*. London, 1992.
Paerssinen, M. *Tawantinsuu*. Helsinki, 1992.
Patterson, T. C. *The Inca Empire*. New York, 1991.
Protzen, J. P. *Inca Architecture and Construction at Ollantaytambo*. New York, 1993.
Stone-Miller, R. *Art of the Andes*. London, 1995.
Zuidman, T. *Inca Civilization in Cuzco*. Austin, 1990.

India in the Middle Ages
Ahir, D. C. *Buddhism in South India*. Delhi, 1992.
Bhattacharyya, N. N. *Buddhism in the History of Indian Ideas*. New Delhi, 1993.
Cook, E., ed. *Light of Liberation*. Berkeley, 1992.
Gonda, J. *A History of Indian Literature*. Wiesbaden, 1984.
Ilangasinha, L. B. *Buddhism in Medieval Sri Lanka*. Delhi, 1992.
Khandalavala, K. *The Golden Age*. Bombay, 1991.
Kulke and Rothermund. *A History of India*. London, 1990.
Pyysiaeinen, J. *Beyond Language and Reason*. Helsinki, 1993.
Sharma, T. R. *A Political History of the Imperial Guptas*. New Delhi, 1989.
Sinor, D., ed. *The Cambridge History of Early Inner Asia*. Cambridge, 1990.
Strong, J. S. *The Legend and Cult of Upagupta*. Princeton, 1992.
Thapar, R. *A History of India, Vol. 1*. Harmondsworth, 1966.

The March of Progress
Brook, T. *Praying for Power*. Cambridge, MA, 1993.
Chan and de Bary, eds. *Yuan Thought*. New York, 1982.
Cotterell, A. *China*. London, 1988.
Ebrey, P. B. *Confucianism and Family Rituals in Imperial China*. Princeton, 1991.
Gernet, J. *Buddhism in Chinese Society*. New York, 1995.
Hyme and Schirokauer. *Ordering the World*. Berkeley, 1993.
Loewe, M. *Crisis and Conflict in Han China*. London, 1974.
Serruys, H. *The Mongols and Ming China*. London, 1987.
Twitchett and Fairbank. *The Cambridge History of China*. Cambridge, 1994.
Twitchett and Wright, eds. *Perspectives on the Tang*. London, 1973.
Waldron, A. *The Great Wall of China*. Cambridge, 1992.
Zurcher, A. *The Buddhist Conquest of China*. Leiden, 1959.

From Kiev to Moscow
Alef, G. *The Origins of Muscovite Autocracy*. Wiesbaden, 1986.
Baron, S. H. *Explorations in Muscovite History*. Hampshire, 1991.

Crummey, R. O. *The Formation of Muscovy*. New York, 1987.

Fennell, J. *The Crisis of Medieval Russia*. New York, 1983.

———. *A History of the Russian Church to 1448*. London, 1995.

Halperin, C. J. *The Tatar Yoke*. Columbus, 1986.

———. *Russia and the Golden Horde*. Bloomington, 1985.

de Hartog, L. *Russia and the Mongol Yoke*. New York, 1996.

Martin, J. *Medieval Russia*. Cambridge, 1995.

Presniakov, A. E. *The Tsardom of Muscovy*. Gulf Breeze, 1978.

Schapov, Y. N. *State and Church in Early Russia*. New York, 1993.

The Emergence of Japan

Bottomley and Hopson. *Arms and Armor of the Samurai*. New York, 1993.

Grossberg, K. A. *Japan's Renaissance*. Cambridge, 1981.

Hall and Takeshi, eds. *Japan in Murumachi Age*. Berkeley, 1977.

Hall, J. W., ed. *The Cambridge History of Japan*. Cambridge, 1988.

Kashiwahara and Sonoda. *Shapers of Japanese Buddhism*. Tokyo, 1994.

Kyohan and Petzold. *The Classification of Buddhism*. Wiesbaden, 1995.

Mass, J. P. *Lordship and Inheritance in Early Medieval Japan*. Stanford, 1989.

———. *The Development of Kamakura Rule*. Stanford, 1979.

Mass, J. P., ed. *Court and Bakufu in Japan*. Princeton, 1982.

Meyer, N. W. *Japan: A Concise History*. Lanham, 1992.

Sansom, G. *A History of Japan*. Stanford, 1982.

The Mongols

DeFrancis, J. *In the Footsteps of Genghis Khan*. Honolulu, 1993.

Halkovic, Jr., S. A. *The Mongols of the West*. Bloomington, 1985.

de Hartog, L. *Genghis Khan, Conqueror of the World*. London, 1989.

Hoang, M. *Genghis Khan*. London, 1990.

Kahn, P. *The Secret History of the Mongols*. San Francisco, 1984.

Morgan, D. *The Mongols*. Oxford, 1986.

Nicolle, D. *The Mongol Warlords*. Poole, 1990.

Onon, U. *The History and the Life of Chinghis Khan*. Leiden, 1990.

Ratchenevsky, P. *Ghenghis Khan*. Oxford, 1991.

Riasanovsky, V. A. *Customary Law of the Mongol Tribes*. Westport, 1979.

Rossabi, M. *Khubilai Khan*. Berkeley, 1988.

The Kingdoms of Africa

Agbodeka, F. *An Economic History of Ghana from the Earliest Times*. Accra, 1992.

Carmichael, J. *African Eldorado*. London, 1993.

Elfasi, M. *Africa from the Seventh to the Eleventh Century*. Berkeley, 1988.

Fage and Oliver. *The Cambridge History of Africa, Vol. I-IV*. Cambridge, 1982.

Levtzion, M. *Ancient Ghana and Mali*. London, 1973.

MacNaughton, P. R. *The Mande Blacksmiths*. Bloomington, 1988.

McKissack and McKissack. *The Royal Kingdoms of Ghana, Mali, and Songhay*. New York, 1994.

Mokhtar, G. *Ancient Civilizations of Africa*. Berkeley, 1990.

Niane, D. T. *Africa from the Twelfth to the Sixteenth Century*. Berkeley, 1984.

Owusu-Ansah and McFarland. *Historical Dictionary of Ghana*. Metuchen, NJ, 1995.

The Advent of the Ottoman Empire

Brummett, P. *Ottoman Seapower and Levantine Diplomacy in the Age of Discovery*. New York, 1994.

Cunt and Woodhead. *Süleyman the Magnificent and His Age*. London, 1995.

Goodwin, G. *The Janissaries*. London, 1994.

Hourani, A. *History of the Arab People*. London, 1991.

Inalcik and Quataert, eds. *An Economic and Social History of the Ottoman Empire*. Cambridge, 1994.

Kortepeter, C. M. *The Ottoman Turcs*. Istanbul, 1991.

Levy, A., ed. *The Jews of the Ottoman Empire*. Princeton, 1994.

Mansfield, P. *A History of the Middle East*. London, 1991.

Pritcher, D. E. *An Historical Geography of the Ottoman Empire from the Earliest Times to the End of the Sixteenth Century*. Leiden, 1972.

Shaw, S. *Empire of the Gazis*. New York, 1970.

Stiles, E. *The Ottoman Empire*. London, 1991.

Illustration Credits

Index

Text is indicated in roman type; illustrations are indicated in italic type.

Svyatoslav 1514, *1514*
Swahili 1551
Swazi kingdom 1554
Syria 1542, 1562, 1574
Szigetvár 1563
Ta-tsi Tsin 1506
Tabasco 1453
Tahuantinsuyu 1480, 1573-1574
Taika *1519*, 1524, 1574; - reforms 1524, 1574
Taira, Japanse clan 1528, 1574
Takauji 1529
Takrur 1545
Talas 1510
Tale of Genji *1524*, 1527
Tamerlane 1497, 1538, *1541-1542*, 1542, 1558, 1573-1574
Tamil 1492-1493
Tampumachay, ruins of 1478
Tamralipti 1500
Tang dynasty *1505*, 1508, 1510, 1526, 1574
Tanganyika Lake 1553
Tangut tribe 1510
Tanzania 1553
Tao (Way of Nature) 1510
Taoism 1508, 1510
Taoist societies 1506
Tapioca 1455
Tarascan 1451-1452
Tarikh as-Sudan 1548
Tarim basin 1504, 1508, 1510
Tartars 1536
Tashkent 1536
Taxila 1500
Technology 1448, 1476, 1574
Temple Major 1471, 1476
Temple of the Sun 1450, 1485
Temples 1447-1448, 1450-1452, 1456, *1464*, 1472, 1476, 1488, 1491, *1493*, 1508, 1573-1574 ;
- of the Cross 1456
Temujin. *See* Genghis Khan
Tenochtitlán (Mexico City) *1460*, 1465-1466, *1467*, 1468-1472, 1474, 1476
Teotihuacán (Place of the Gods) 1450-1451, *1451*, 1456, *1464*, *1466*, 1471, 1574
Tepanecs 1465-1466, 1468-1469
Tepantitla Palace 1450
Teponaztli 1452
Terracing *1448*, 1480
Texcoco 1465-1466, 1574
Tezcatlipoca 1471
Theology 1560
Thessalonica 1559
Third Rome (Moscow) 1518
Thomas Aquinas, Saint 1561
Thrace 1556, 1573
Three Kingdoms, period in Chinese history 1506, 1574
Tibet 1508, 1537-1538, 1540, 1574
Tihuanaco *1452*, 1479, 1480, 1574
Tikai (Guatemala) 1454
Tikal *1455*, 1456, *1464*
Timbuktu 1545, 1547-1548
Timur. *See* Tamerlane
Timur Lang (Timur the Lame) 1542
Timurid dynasty 1542
Timurlenk. *See* Tamerlane
Titicaca, lake 1452, 1574
Tiwanaku 1452, 1483
Tizoc 1469
Tlachtli (ritual ball game) 1451
Tlacopan 1465-1466

Tlahuizcalpantecuhtli, Temple of 1451
Tlalocan (water goddess) 1450
Tlapacoya 1450
Tlatecuhtli (earth monster) 1471
Tlatoani, Aztec king 1468, 1470, 1573-1574
Todaiji Temple 1523
Togrul Beg 1555, 1564
Tokyo 1520
Toltecs 1451, *1451*, 1458, 1465, 1468, *1474*, 1574
Tomb culture 1520
Tombe civilization (300–800) 1574
Tombs 1448, 1451, 1464, 1522, 1543, 1545
Tonatiuh (sun god) *1470*, 1471, 1573
Tonga people 1554
Tonkin 1504, 1540
Topa Inca Yupanqui 1478
Toramana 1491
Totonac 1451
Toulouse 1561
Trans-Saharan trade 1550
Transoxania (Uzbekistan) 1542
Tribute 1465-1466, 1469-1471, 1476, 1491, 1510, 1516, 1518, 1534, 1536, 1538, 1542, 1557, 1573-1574
Tripoli 1548, 1562
Tsai-lun 1506, 1574
Tsnao Tsnao, Han general (155–220) 1506
Tughluq dynasty (1325–1351) 1497
Tughluqs 1496-1497
Tula 1451, 1465, *1474*, 1574
Tulum 1458
Tupac Amaru 1480;
- Yupanqui 1574
Tupu 1486
Turkestan 1508, 1532, 1536, 1538, 1547, 1556, 1574
Turkic nomads 1515
Turkish Empire 1536, 1558-1559, 1566
Turkmenistan 1539
Turko-Afghan dynasties 1496
Tutsi 1553
Tver 1518
Tzimpo 1557
Tzintzuntzan 1452
Tzompantli 1451
Uaxactún 1456
Uji 1523-1524, 1574
Ukraine 1514, 1574
Ulama 1458, 1462, 1562, 1574
Umako (d.626) 1524
Ummayad (661–750) 1494
Ural River 1536
Urubamba River 1488
Usamacinta River Basin 1456
Uxmal 1456
Valdayskaya Hills 1513
Varangians 1514
Varna, Battle of (1444) 1559
Vasco de Balboa (1475–1519) 1477
Veche 1517
Venezuela 1447
Vera Cruz 1451, 1453
Victoria Lake 1553
Vicuna 1449
Vienna 1563, 1566
Vietnam 1504, 1508
Vijayanagar, Hindu kingdom founded in 1336 1497
Viracocha (the Creator), Inca emperor (fifteenth century) 1478-1479, *1479*, 1483, 1574
Vishnu (god) 1496

Vladimir-Suzdal region 1516, 1536
Vladimir the Great (Vladimir I), king of Kyyivan (980–1015) *1513*, 1514-1517, 1574
Volga 1513, 1516, 1542, 1574
Volhynia 1516
Volkhov 1513
Volta 1551
Wadai 1549
Wahlstatt 1536
Wai Wang 1535
Wang Mang 1504-1505
Wangara Region 1545
Warring States period (1467–1568) 1520, 1530, 1573-1574
Warriors, Temple of the 1457
Wei 1506, 1508, 1574;
- kingdom (453–225 BC) 1506
Wene, Kongo king 1553
Western Hemisphere 1450
White Huns 1491, 1574
Wladyslaw III (1456–1516) 1559
World War I (1914–1918) 1556, 1574
World War II (1940–1945) 1563
Wroclaw 1536
Wu (222–280) 1504, 1506, 1574
Wu-ti, emperor of the Han dynasty (140–86 BC) 1504, 1506, 1574
Xhosa 1554
Yüan, dynastic title 1512, 1541;
- dynasty, Mongol dynasty 1512, 1541-1542
Yablonovy 1531
Yagul 1452
Yamashiro 1530
Yamato Empire 1524, 1574;
- Plain 1523, 1574
Yanaconas 1484-1485, 1574
Yang Chien 1508
Yangtze Valley 1512, 1542
Yarhisar 1556
Yaroslav the Wise *1513*, 1515-1517, 1574
Yayoi civilization 1520, 1530, 1574
Yellow River 1504
Yellow Turbans 1506
Yemen 1544
Yenisehir 1556
Yenking (Beijing) 1535
Yesukai 1532
Yian dynasty 1574
Yildirim. *See* Bayezid I
Yoritomo Minamoto 1528, 1574
Yoruba tribe 1551, 1553
Yoshino 1529
Yuan dynasty (1279–1368) 1574
Yucatán 1451, 1453, 1456-1458
Yugoslavia 1563
Yupanqui. *See* Capac; Cusi; Tupac
Zagwe 1544
Zaire 1550
Zakat, payment of 1566
Zambezi River 1553
Zambia 1554
Zanzibar 1551
Zapotec *1447*, 1451, *1474*, 1573
Zaques 1573
Zaria 1550
Zenith 1491
Zimbabwe 1553-1554
Zipas 1573
Zulu 1554
Zulumfecane (1830–1840) 1554
Zwangendaba, African king 1553-1554

Text is indicated in roman type; illustrations are indicated in italic type.